Giotto's Venetian Moor

RANDOLPH STARN

ORIN STARN

Na maravegia sola no la xe mai bastanza.
Just a single miracle is never enough.

1

It is Tuesday, March 12, 1336. At the break of day the old man's boatmen row him across the lagoon to Murano. He sits, stooped and wrinkled, under the sleek boat's brocade canopy. A fine wool blanket lies over his lap against the late winter chill. The boat cuts through the still green waters under a heavy sky threatening to snuff out the pale light. Only the rhythmic dipping of the oars and the fretful cry of wheeling seabirds break the silence.

The old man has chosen his destination carefully. The five linked islands of Murano are like Venice in miniature but without its distractions. The monastery of San Mattia stands on the far edge of the island cluster, turned away from the watery metropolis on the horizon. The monks are accustomed to opening this shelter to the rich and well-born. Alliances are made, contracts signed, documents sealed there with their blessing.

Thirty-four witnesses have gathered in the monastery's great hall. The glow and glitter of mosaic and Murano glass suit the distinguished company of churchmen and scions of prominent families from Venice and the mainland. Some are already seated, others stand expectantly; they nod to one another with the quiet condescension of privilege. As the old man enters, the prior steps forward to greet him with the sign of the cross: "Welcome in peace and the name of the Lord, Messer Enrico. May our prayers for you be granted here and in the hereafter." Two white-robed monks guide him to a gilded chair at the table where his notaries wait, parchment and quills at the ready.

The touch of gold pleases him. People say it pleases him only too much, that he, Enrico Scrovegni, will suffer the torments of the damned that a family of usurers deserves. Cretins! Let them mind their own affairs. He will show how a rich man passes through the needle's eye into paradise. Gold is not his greatest treasure. The church he built for the Madonna in Padua is. It rises over the ruins of the ancient arena, redeeming blood-soaked pagan ground and mocking the petty tyrant who forced him into exile. He has filled this true treasure chest with ransom for his soul and the admiration of heaven and earth—altars, relics, images. His last will and testament will seal his bid on the future.

He smiles to himself at the law's contrivances. The plodding legal Latin lends solemn dignity to the desires of this world. The polished parchment of the notaries, four of them, is inscribed in Christ's name with his worldly titles: *prudent and noble Knight, Lord Enrico of the Scrovegni, son of Lord Raynaldo Scrovegni, Citizen of Padua and of Venice.* So much for the fools who snicker that the Scrovegni name, "pregnant sows," suits an upstart race of money lenders.

He has bought off that bad joke many times over. Everybody knows that the big money in Padua comes from loaning it. The city fathers are happy to get as much of it as they can and the priests absolve whatever sin there may be in making money, for a price. That arrogant scribbler Dante put his father Raynaldo in hell with the usurers scratching their fleas like mad dogs. Ungrateful beggar. Dead for fifteen years, he'll not be imagining by now how Hell punishes the likes of him.

Im primis ego Enricus Scrovegnus—the Latin, more direct now, breaks into his reveries: "In the first place I, Enrico Scrovegni, want my body buried in the church and monument I made and paid for in Padua." Yes, he wants care for his body joined with care of his soul. The scholars at the university in Padua like to argue with their texts and glosses about bodies and souls, but he has not separated them in life and does not mean to do so in his ultimate transaction. The scholars speculate; he acts so that things of the body provide for the good of the soul. He assigns bequests to the Madonna of Charity of the Arena and many other churches and convents, alms for the poor and amends for rightful creditors. Finally, provisions for his heirs and executors. They can afford to wait.

If the devil lies in the details, the notaries will beat the Evil One at his own game. Their formulas are exacting. Ill-gotten gains? His own and his family's besides? Let them be restored—if anyone making claims can prove them. Let many donations to the religious and the poor be made from properties rightfully his—before they were stolen by Marsiglio da Carrara, whose treachery drove him into exile in Venice more than fifteen years earlier. Let that tyrant confront his crimes in the just petitions of those who appeal to him in the honorable name of Enrico Scrovegni. Where is the devil in these details?

The last clauses come late in the day. The law never hurries over death. His witnesses have come and gone. Some are in debt to him, some have expectations of a reward. But all those assembled have done their duty, vouching for the worth of the old man in this world and the next. Like everything else in Venice, the ritual is a measure of their own standing.

The old man feels a surge of weary satisfaction at having outwitted death one more time as his oarsmen steer his boat back to the crimson and purple city floating in the sunset.

***

Regina Payne cradled a glass of cool white Verduzzo at the window of her little apartment with its glimpse of the Grand Canal. The sunset's purple, gold, and crimson were performing their spectacular evening ritual. Church bells, grinding vaporetto engines, the shouts of boatmen across the waterway blended into a soundtrack for a parade of palace facades. At moments like this Regina didn't care if anything she could say about Venice had been said already. Probably countless times. The clichés never got it quite right and they contradicted one another anyway.

These days serious people were supposed to complain about the sorry state of the sinking city. As a graduate student in art history Regina was not sure that she counted as a serious person, or that she wanted to be if that meant thinking you really understood the sheer improbability of the place.

Just then, her phone buzzed with a text from her Venetian friend Flavia. "*Caffè Rosso alle sette?*—Caffè Rosso at 7?" Flavia was an architecture student she had met at the biannual architecture show that alternated with the better-known *Biennale* for art. While they were waiting in line at the entrance to the exhibits in the old Venetian Arsenal, Flavia had volunteered that the arsenal building complex was the real sensation of the show. "You know, it's a factory, shipyard, harbor, fortress, monument all in one; do you think celebrity architects now could do anything like that?" You never had to guess what Flavia thought about something. She was an exception to the tight circles of family and neighborhood in Venice and she had become Regina's trusty guide to insider's knowledge that outsiders missed.

It was still balmy outside when Regina took the *traghetto*, the gondola ferry, across the Grand Canal from Cannaregio to meet Flavia. This was no faster than circling around on foot over the Rialto bridge, but she enjoyed the gondola ride and the gondoliers too. They took shifts in pairs ferrying passengers across the busy waterway with a few deft strokes, charging Venetians one euro and everyone else twice that. The young gondoliers looked the cheesecake part with their ribboned straw hats, striped shirts, and the jaunty confidence that came with being the world's most iconic boatmen. Regina had sent a copy of the hunky "Gondoliers of Venice" calendar to her gay friend Tim for his birthday, with a promise to send the companion "Priests of Venice" next time. She smiled back over her shoulder at the taller of the two boatmen who eyed her appreciatively after helping her onto the swaying wooden dock.

It was a serious compliment when there were so many erotic treats vying for their attention. She didn't do glam, but a young black woman who was not a grungy American tourist or an African dressed in dashiki was a rarity that kept the Venetians guessing. Regina liked it that way. She was fine with being noticed—she didn't have much choice in any case—but she was not a show-off. Her skin was in-between dark and light; she wore her hair short and dressed in silvery beige and white and soft colors; her angular slenderness made her look taller than she was. Her dark eyes and high brow conveyed more self-assurance than she actually felt. Anyway, she wasn't especially shy and was, she thought, sexy enough without having to advertise it.

Making her way through the usual twists and turns to Campo Santa Margherita she found Flavia already waiting at an outside table at the Caffè Rosso. It was a laid back remnant of the old Bohemian scene and Campo Santa Margherita was one of the largest squares in Venice but a safe distance across the Grand Canal from the tourist Bermuda Triangle around San Marco. Students from the university nearby at Ca' Foscari hung out there; on this night there were some artsy locals and the very Italian scene of a few boys kicking around a soccer ball. It was a comfortable place to meet your friends and snoop on strangers over drinks and gossip. It was still a bargain too, even in Venice and even with a front row seat.

Flavia ordered the regulation Venetian Aperol Spritz for them both. It tasted like spiked orange Kool-Aid to Regina, but she accepted this as part of her assimilation ritual. Flavia raised her glass. "I know you think it tastes like medicine. That suits me today. They're laying us off at the Gesuati." Flavia worked part time as an art restorer to finance her off-and-on studies at IUAV, the Institute of Architecture.

"It's OK about the Gesuati, though. Clammy church, long hours, scary scaffolds. The pay is bad even before the bosses skim off their cut. Anyway, graduating wouldn't land me a good job. Too many graduates in line already."

Regina was sympathetic and then some. "I may be in a line like that. Or working somewhere in a Renaissance theme park. Maybe Las Vegas—the Hotel Venetian?" She was trying to humor Flavia, but she was not joking. The Renaissance was big business as a corporate brand and a tacky entertainment. But Renaissance hotel chains and the fake learning of Dan Brown novels had no use for real scholars and the art world was hooked on the latest fads.

"Maybe so," Flavia said. "But you've got a grant to be in this real theme park. Not bad, I'd say."

Flavia was right. Regina had beaten the odds, so far. She didn't come from an academic family, unless you counted her father's high school history teaching and her mother's library job. As a girl she loved looking at the art books on the shelves in the big library where her mother worked, most of all the mix of real and ideal that she found beguiling in Renaissance art. She began tracing Renaissance pictures, then drew from them, observing the world and imagining worlds of her own making. Her parents didn't object so long as she kept up her grades; the friends she cared about ribbed her about all those nudes and virgins, but they got used to this "weird Regina thing."

It might have been a passing fancy but for the life-changing fluke of a teacher and mentor at Spelman, her mother's alma mater. Marjorie Robbins was an outlier with her passion for Renaissance painting and all the more committed for that reason. She spent as much time she could manage in Italy, photographing art work for her classes, well known pieces but out-of-the-way finds too. She had written a dissertation and published articles on the painter Domenico Veneziano. "Not a big name in the 15th-century painting Pantheon," she told her class on "visual culture," a shiny new label, she said mischievously, that was best studied in the old art. "But Domenico's fascinating really, a migratory bird of a painter who goes from Venice—that's where the name Veneziano comes from—to Florence, Perugia, and Rome. You can see him mixing Venetian color and Florentine line. There's some racy art scandal too: a rival supposedly murdered him."

The mix of straightforwardness and enthusiasm was irresistible. Marjorie took it for granted that Regina would apply for the junior year abroad program in Florence and that her parents would be persuaded by the honor and the financial aid when Regina was accepted. "You'll be staying with my art restorer friend Giulia of course. Full-time immersion that way. Your own Renaissance."

It had apparently never occurred to her for a minute that Regina would not learn Italian quickly, take classes at the Accademia, and intern with her friends at a conservation lab in Florence. Still more surprising, that was pretty much what had happened. It came together with an honors thesis on Giotto's great Ognissanti altarpiece in the Uffizi Gallery. Regina doted on the solidly regal Mary and her Christ child prince on a throne with the angel choir ringed around them. After time off to work at the High Museum in Atlanta, she set aside the odds against a career in medieval and Renaissance art history. Alerted to the snobbishness of Ivy League graduate programs and the Institute of Fine Art and to the disarray at Berkeley, she applied to Duke and was accepted.

"I'm sorry, Flavia. I didn't mean to sound like I was complaining."

"It's OK. You probably just need to recharge."

"I don't know. I'm supposed to be working on the Bellini family as—what?—as a production team of Venetian painters with connections as far away as Istanbul. That's what my adviser signed off on." John Terterian was a rising star in the market for new-style art history; he had encouraged Regina to delve into the economic and social networks of Renaissance art-making. She would be updating the old-style art history that way, which was, after all, what the Bellini did.

"But is that really what *you* want to do? Maybe you should press the pause button. Take a break. Go over to Padua, to the Arena Chapel. It'll be like going back to a first love. You think you know about Giotto already, but when you're there you discover things. Just go, *cara*. Even with the crowds, it's *una figata pazzesca*—fucking amazing."

***

The long day on Murano had exhausted him. It was already well past dark by the time his boat glided up to the Ca' Scrovegni near the church of San Maurizio. Almost every residence had its own dock and water gate in a city of winding canals. Even the most palatial of habitations were called *Case*, "houses." Only the elected head of the Republic, the Doge, was entitled to live in a "palace." Scrovegni had to learn these subtle Venetian codes of false modesty and political prudence. There was nothing modest or prudent about the great palace he had built in Padua and was forced to leave behind.

As he was helped from the boat, the old man's giant shadow in the torchlight mocked the fragility he felt. In times past he would have climbed straightaway to the long hall on the first floor and surveyed the flickering lights of traffic on the canals from its loggia. He would have listened to the news of the day and welcomed an evening's guests. Wives and children in Venice, if they appeared at all, would have soon retired to the family quarters. His second marriage to Iacobina d'Este brought what he wanted most in a wife—the prestige of her ruling family in Ferrara and two sons. There were other ways of enjoying female company and the pleasures of the flesh. He had indulged in the caresses, the music, and the conversation of the women who made a profession of it.

It was so cold that he could see his breath even with the fireplace stoked in his high-ceilinged bedroom. Glowing carpets from the East, the carved chests, the hangings of tapestries and pictures in gilded frames were shadows in his faded eyes as he shuffled towards the canopied bed with its thick goose down quilt. No matter how tired his body was, he had trouble falling asleep nowadays or staying asleep for long. His restlessness had made him a rich man with ambitions that were not limited to money, and now his mind was fitfully whirling through his provisions for the future.

Only as he slipped toward sleep did his thoughts wander back in time. He took some comfort recalling his last celebration of the Feast of the Annunciation at home in Padua. A buzzing crowd had gathered to the roll of drums and trumpet blasts in the piazza that was the heart of the city. From the balcony arcade circling the city hall he had looked out over the fluttering banners with the insignia and colors of city officials, clergy, knights, guildsmen, neighborhoods. The herald had invited him with the bishop and the city magistrates to take their appointed places. Two curly-headed children, looking embarrassed and pleased as a miniature Virgin Annunciate and an Archangel Gabriel, led the procession out of the piazza down the cobbled streets, past the cathedral and on to Santa Maria della Carità dell'Arena.

Phrases from its dedication flickered through the old man's mind:

> *Enrico Scrovegni, knight, prompted by his honest soul has caused this temple built in this place to be dedicated to the Mother of God.... In recompense to enjoy eternal grace.... Divine virtue has thus taken the place of profane vices, conferring celestial joy on the otherwise useless things of the earth.*

True, the Venetians had made him a citizen, "for his merits" according to the official decree with its gilded seal. That was a rare honor for an outsider. For all their trumpeting about their "most serene" republic, the *Serenissima,* as mistress of the seas, capital of an empire, market for the four quarters of the compass, the Venetians were attentive to differences and closed in on themselves while calculating the price of everything. Scrovegni's loans to merchants with patrician names and investments in public bonds and his daughter's dowries were proof enough for the Venetians of "his merits." But that did not make him one of them. He knew as well as they did that he would never be the big fish in the lagoon that he had been in the slow-moving rivers Brenta and Bacchiglione in Padua.

And it was still Padua that he cared the most about. Of all things there, the church at the Arena. In his will *my church* came first and, as his intended burial place, last.

He had lived in exile nearly twenty years. A fine reward for guarding his reputation at home. He had spoken circumspectly in the city councils, joined a society of pious laymen, contributed generous alms and offerings. Steering carefully between factions, he had taken a Carrara woman as his first wife while Marsiglio da Carrara married a Scrovegni.

A lot of good it had done him. Marsigilo had disposed of the Scrovegni wife with poison; after that he had seen to the execution of two Scrovegni cousins, with the mercy of the sword, he snarled, instead of the gallows they deserved. That snake in the grass lied to confiscate as much Scrovegni property as he could lay his hands on. One undeserved misfortune after another.

But fortunes could change, and probably would with the conniving bad faith of the Carrara clan. They were a foul race of tyrants no matter how many fancy titles they bragged about and mostly stole for themselves.

Scrovegni's will anticipated his coming home in a magnificent tomb that he commissioned to be erected in his church. He relished the thought of his effigy presiding from the altar over the cunning pictures on lower register of the walls. That was where *his* virtues mocked *their* perverse opposites: Stupidity, Inconstancy, Anger, Injustice, Envy, and Despair. Stories of the Virgin and her Son unfolded around the upper walls as a Bible in pictures for everyone to recognize and take to heart. But he meant the figures of virtues and vices below them to provoke and to condemn. They were disguised in paint to look like carvings in stone; the virtues of Prudence, Fortitude, Temperance, Justice, Faith, Charity, and Hope silently denounced their villainous contraries on the wall across from them. In the very center of the virtues Justice presided, entitled to her throne; opposite her, Injustice was crime and war's twisted tyrant. It had pleased him to hear learned men argue about the higher meaning of images that were his personal justification and revenge.

His will did not mention the Arena pictures. No one would have expected it to. The pictures were fixed in fresco and there was no need to write about what was *his* work. Painters were hired hands. They might try to get away with substitutes for blue ultramarine or red vermilion that cost more than gold, but the work was cheap. Especially painting in fresco. The first plaster layer was shop boys' dirty work, thick and rough so as to bond with the wall and smoother layers on top of it. The last layer was pigment painted on patches of fresh plaster before it dried, one day at a time, from the top of a wall to the bottom. It all belonged to him, even when Giotto was in charge.

And even when stories about Giotto had spread far and wide. It was said he had been discovered one warm Tuscan afternoon when the painter Cimabue, out for a country walk, happened upon him as a shepherd boy sketching a sheep with a stone on a flat rock. The painter was so smitten that he arranged with the boy's father to take him on as an apprentice in his workshop in Florence.

Pope Boniface, never one to mince words, had summoned Giotto to work in Rome for the Jubilee Year he proclaimed in 1300: "Since the Lord has granted this squat, ugly Tuscan the grace to make beautiful things, We shall let His will be done." Another story came from Boniface's successor. This Benedict XI had exchanged favors with the Scrovegni when he was still a bishop in nearby Treviso. Nicola Boccasini was his name; the higher he rose the more forgetful of his vows he became. It had cost Boniface his life to believe he could beat the king of France at extortion. It was said that the old sinner killed himself by beating his head against the wall of the cell where the French locked him up. That sounded like him, raging even in death. As if hellfire were not enough, the French put his memory on trial. Boccasini had the French to worry about, but the first thing he did as Pope Benedict was to send out messengers to bring the best painters to Rome.

When one of them came to Giotto's workshop, Giotto took a red chalk and drew a perfect circle freehand. "Take this to the Holy Father," he said.

"But what else?" the messenger asked.

"It will be enough."

And it had been for the pope. For Enrico Scrovegni too.

He and Giotto had tested one another with the story when they discussed the Arena project to which Papa Boccasini had given his blessing with the promise of special privileges.

"So, Master Giotto, my friend from Treviso saw through your little joke. The poor messenger thought you were only showing off the skill of your hand. Any painter worth his salt could have done that."

"Certainly, Messer Enrico, either making a circle or any perfect figure."

"It could have been a square then."

Giotto smiled. "This is perhaps your little joke, Signore? What could be more perfect than the circle in God's creation? He made it unchanging, the form of the spheres of heaven, the figure of time beginning in Adam and closing with the Last Judgment."

"I see your wit equals your brush, Master Giotto. Let us find out how you will paint the vault of heaven with God the Father over the story of the Virgin and her Son and the Judgment at the end. You shall have everything you need so that this church of mine triumphs, even over the ancients."

And so that I, Enrico Scrovegni, shall be seen there at the head of the elect, triumphant in Paradise.

On the wall of the Last Judgment he kneels, the young man he once was, only finer and fairer in the fullness he expects to enjoy again at the Resurrection. He offers a model of his church to the Madonna and her haloed companions. Her hand reaches toward his, as if to receive a gesture of blessing that is rightly hers to give. He takes pride of place ahead of the legions of the saved, larger than any of them; his gaze, like theirs, is shielded from the horrors of the damned when Christ shall return to judge the living and the dead. The painted stories from the life of the Virgin and her Son circle round the walls under the starry blue vault as if unfurled by his upraised hand.

***

Santa Lucia was a good patron saint for changing places. Regina hurried for a quick stand-up cappuccino and a brioche before boarding the train at the station named after her. Lucy's body had gone from Sicily to Constantinople; it was stolen by the Venetians—one more trophy saint—and she moved again when her namesake church was torn down to make way for the station in one of the seizures of modernization that periodically gripped Venice. Flavia's suggestion over a drink in Campo Santa Margherita that she go to Padua and reconnect with Giotto had sounded like a dare; it became a temptation during a restless night and felt now like a welcome relief.

It was more or less half an hour to Padua, depending on the train, but it was a different world across the bridge over the lagoon. The view from the window looked like a movie trailer for an industrial dystopia. Flavia had talked about some relatives moving to Mestre on the mainland in the 80's. "Just in time to get screwed twice over. They sold the old family apartment to an American expat and landed in the shithole of pollution and corruption. That's what 'Save Venice' meant back then."

The jerry-built shopping mall inside the Padua station did nothing to improve its shabby look. A few faded posters bravely saluted Padua's historical sites and the most famous heroes of its ancient university, Copernicus and Galileo. There was not much else to show that Padua had been a thriving medieval republic and a prize for a rogues gallery of petty princes before the Venetians took it over in the 15th century.

All Regina saw outside the station was a profusion of transit stops and the routine *Viale Garibaldi* of a provincial Italian town. She had been warned that "provincial town" would be fighting words for people who lived in one. Towns in Italy had been "countries" for centuries when an Italian "state" was still a pipe dream and, to many ways of thinking, a nightmare. The Paduans actually had claims to a more serious Renaissance than the Florentines who were more unscrupulous and persistent at self-promotion.

Regina wanted to feel solid ground under her feet and find out if she could still manage the daredevil sport of dodging Italian traffic. She followed the *Viale Garibaldi* for a noisy quarter of a mile before crossing an incongruous triumphal monument of a bridge over a sluggish canal. A fleet of tour buses was lined up at the main entrance to the chapel some distance ahead, but she came to a small gate in a low fence of rusty iron stakes. When no one appeared to shoo her away, she ducked through the gate into a grassy open space in the jumbled remains of the ancient Roman arena that gave the chapel its formal title, Santa Maria della Carità dell'Arena.

And there it was. It looked very much like it did in Giotto's famous scene of Enrico Scrovegni presenting a miniature chapel to the Virgin Mary. The model always reminded Regina of a doll's house, but the pink brick rectangle with its pitched roof really was small and unadorned. It was an orphan too, without the huge family palace Scrovegni had built beside it to leave no doubt about who was making the connection between piety and the world. A Venetian family that inherited the property tore it down early in the 19th century. Regina's guidebook noted tersely that the patrician vandals would have demolished the chapel too if it didn't fall down first. Without putting it in so many words, the guidebook said that British bombs had come perilously close to finishing the job in World War II.

To get in Regina had to go through the main entrance and the inevitable souvenir shop before coming to a glare-white plastic counter to pick up the ticket she had reserved. It was not clear that she needed one since she had a researcher's pass, but she had been told that reservations were necessary and had given up trying to second guess the rules. Italy was anything but consistent about its art treasures. Some politicians were all for privatization; she saw a TV comic sniping at museums as "a geriatric burden." Museum officials held forth in platitudes about "our responsibility to protect a sacred legacy," particularly when some scandalous oversight came to light. Regina was shocked to see a paunchy British tourist reach out to stroke Donatello's bronze David in the Bargello museum in Florence without the bored guard even noticing. "You know," she had said with an aggressive smile, "it says not to touch the art for a reason." The man had slunk away in embarrassment; the guard shrugged.

The Scrovegni set-up was obviously meant to be a redeeming showpiece of modern scientific management. There was a pressurized entry chamber to control air pollution and humidity. Only 25 people at a time were allowed in the chapel for a fifteen-minute stretch. Regina waited her turn with a group that marveled at the technology she thought would be more suited to a spaceship. When the sealed glass door slid open, she walked with the others up the short passageway that opened into the chapel.

Ahead of her, a guide raised his furled umbrella to summon his flock and launched into his set piece. "Some of you—raise your hands, if you please—have seen the Sistine Chapel in Rome, no? And have marveled— have you not?—at the stupendous frescoes of Michelangelo?" The guide twirled the umbrella. "Here we have northern Italy's Sistine at the very dawn of the Renaissance."

Just leave the Sistine out of it, Regina said to herself. She had a friendly argument once—at least she thought it was friendly—with someone about Michelangelo's ceiling. She found the figures bombastic, their strained poses and bulging muscles resentfully subservient to the forced show of Michelangelo's theatrics. The viewer had to twist, strain, and squint to see them. She couldn't imagine them able to walk, talk, or feel outside the script of creation, sin, and salvation. "I'll take the Arena figures over Michelangelo's any day," she had concluded, thinking she had clinched the argument.

She still thought so. For her honors thesis with Marjorie Robbins and in a graduate student boot camp on Italian Renaissance painting, she had read whole shelves of Giotto studies. She could recite the "Giotto Drill" in her sleep: Giotto the Father of Renaissance Art; Giotto's Three Dimensions, Naturalism, and Expressive Feeling dispelling the rigid hierarchies, the gold and ritual distance of Byzantine and medieval painting; Giotto the Founding Father of the Renaissance Revolution in Time and

Space. But formulas and labels couldn't do justice to the real thing and the sheer presence of the space itself.

Regina held her breath—*as if that would help to take it all in,* she thought; *probably no one since Giotto has done that.* Turning to the long walls, she followed the bands of narrative from the lives of Mary and Jesus. She knew her Bible from her southern girlhood. Her parents had taken her every Sunday to the Baptist church downtown. She never could quite bring herself to believe, even as a girl. But her Bible Belt upbringing and her resistance to it fed into her fascination with the serious religion and serious worldliness of the Renaissance.

She knew that the almost painful directness of the Bible stories on the walls was an illusion, but the figures acting out their assigned roles were uncannily expressive, their simplicity not simple at all. Regina imagined them wanting her to surrender her art historian's cool. The up-to-date thing was to see Giotto not so much as the founding genius of Renaissance art but as Giotto Inc., the corporate executive of a for-hire workshop. Scholars still used the R-word—"Renaissance"—but by and large apologetically or defensively; their jobs depended on it. But it seemed stingily academic to resist the genius in the tenderness of the meeting of old couple, Joachim and Anna, expecting the seemingly miraculous birth of Mary; the joy of the angels at the manger in Bethlehem; the sleepy obliviousness of the Apostle John at the Last Supper; Judas's treachery with his pinched kiss of Jesus and his menacing yellow cloak; Mary's devastation over the punctured corpse just off the cross.

The title of a book Regina had seen in a bookstore window came to mind: *L'affare migliore di Enrico: Giotto e la Capella Scrovegni,* "Enrico's Best Deal: Giotto and the Scrovegni Chapel." Scrovegni had appeared not once but three times in the chapel: as a young man in a full length sculpture that may have stood originally in an outside niche; as a recumbent old man attended by angels in the marble of his tomb behind the main altar; as the perfected man offering the chapel to the Virgin at the head of the legion of souls destined for resurrection in the stupendous Last Judgment. A good deal for sure.

Looking over the railing at Giotto's Scrovegni portrait Regina was not persuaded he was the fearful penitent whose atonement for the sin of usury explained why he commissioned the chapel. That was one of the latest theories, but in his rich man's violet robe and hat trimmed with white fur Scrovegni looked more self-satisfied and entitled than guilty of anything. He certainly wasn't shy about celebrating himself or about getting his money's worth. Regina didn't feel it was at all irreverent to think of insider trading and rigged business deals. That's the way patronage worked: patrons commissioned art for churches expecting favors in return. Not many would have had a Giotto working for them, but even Giotto was a hired hand and so were the saints whose images were sometimes whitewashed and replaced if they failed to deliver.

"Cinque minuti—five minutes left." The guard's warning always came too soon. Each of Giotto's thirty narratives called for more time than anyone could give them. But Flavia was right to say that that you discovered different things in them no matter how much or how little time you had.

One figure in particular riveted Regina's attention this time. In the Flagellation scene Jesus, bound and soon to be crucified, sat to one side in a mock regal robe with blood trickling from his crown of thorns. On the other side, sinister priests and officials in togas gestured, commanding punishment, humiliation, and a death sentence as a clutch of ruffians taunted and beat him in anticipation. A figure in the center between the two groups raised a stick as if meaning to strike the helpless Jesus. Or maybe not. The gesture looked indecisive, suspended, ambivalent, but there was nothing ambiguous about the look of the figure: he was the only black man among the hundreds of figures painted in the chapel, a man with dark chocolate-colored skin.

As usual in Italy's museums, Regina was the only black person in the chapel. Her attraction to the Renaissance, a badge of honor conferred by Marjorie Robbins, cut against the unspoken academic racial profiling for black graduate students. They were expected to work on art in Africa or the black diaspora or some neglected or forgotten black artist. In Venice she hadn't paid much attention to the bronze figures of the Moors—a common European name for black people—that struck the bells on the Renaissance clock tower in the Piazza San Marco. Walkways and courtyards labeled "Moro" blended easily into the cityscape, and images identified as "Mori" in churches, palaces, and museums were routine exoticism in a city that was full of it. But the black tormentor, if that was what he was meant to be, was different. He was Giotto's Moor, singular in Scrovegni's chapel, a figure who did not fit what Regina knew about the limited stock of black people in the art of Giotto's time—one of the Three Wisemen, an emperor of Ethiopia, the Queen of Sheba, or, more common, a cartoonish villain. This figure of Giotto's stood at a peculiar remove from the other figures, almost as if he were not there by choice, halting, as if not ready to strike, his expression in profile more distracted than intent on the business at hand.

The buzzer didn't respect these reflections or anything else. It sounded like a police alarm. A pair of guards ushered Regina's group out of the pressurized glass cage to bring in the next contingent. She made a note to herself to do some investigating. She didn't know what she expected to find, only that she wanted to know more about Giotto's Moor.

It had turned into a lovely sunny day outside, perfect for taking a stroll around the old part of Padua. She circled to the church of *Il Santo*—no one had to be told that it was Sant'Antonio's church. Donatello's monumental equestrian statue of the Renaissance warlord Gattamelata, the Honey Cat, guarded the plain Franciscan façade and served as a decoy for flocks of pigeons. The domes on the roof and the treasures inside were anything but plain. The saint's relics drew long lines of pilgrims past painting, sculpture, and silver to touch the green stone on his sarcophagus. Old Italian ladies, stiff northerners, self-conscious Americans, immigrant Sudanese street vendors, all alike hoped for favors from the saint.

Saint Anthony was the patron saint for finding lost people or things. Regina's Baptist relatives back home would be shocked, but she thought she would like to light a candle: *So, Antonio, what about a back story for Giotto's Moor?*

***

Enrico Scrovegni lay in bed with his eyes wide open. He wondered if he had slept. The leaded glass windows shut out the sounds of wind and slapping water. But the household clatter had begun with wood being split down in the kitchen. A rooster began its piercing alarm to make the sun rise. The sky would soon be flaming behind the domes of San Marco.

The manservant knowing his master's habits and anticipating his needs rose from his straw pallet. He lit a wall torch and stoked the embers of the fire, then laid out his master's clothes for the day: tights and breeches, the belt with the gold buckle, the woolen cloak and scarf, the head cloth.

"Ah, Lionardo, the night was so long," Scrovegni said, almost in a whisper. He needed help in pulling the tights over his sagging flesh. He had been handsome in his youth, almost as Giotto painted him, and he still tried to maintain appearances—a *bella figura*. More important now, the warm pressure of the finely-woven tights of shimmering cochineal Hangzhou silk eased his pain.

"I have forgotten how to sleep." Lionardo knew that his master had never rested quietly, even years ago when they were both young. He had been sold into Scrovegni's service at the age of seventeen, in the beginning as an exotic curiosity dressed up in his master's livery. Lionardo's family had been dispersed when the old emperor's elite Moorish garrison in the south of Italy was rooted out for the honor of Christendom and the much greater satisfaction of the emperor's enemies. Scrovegni made Lionardo one of the bodyguards that he, like all the big men in Padua, flaunted for prestige and needed for protection. He had accompanied his master in exile to Venice, by that time as a trusted member of the household.

"You will wish to attend mass, Signore?" Lionardo asked, knowing that it would take more than a bad night to keep Scrovegni from his routines.

The bells had just begun the call to first mass. Lionardo helped his master down the stairs from the living quarters of Ca' Scrovegni and out to the embankment leading toward the church of San Maurizio.

The mixed sounds of night and the coming day echoed in the semi-darkness. A few drunks staggered home after a night's carousing; a porter shouted out to get by with his push cart stacked high with firewood. The air stank. The tide had not yet flushed the city's sludge and stink out to the Adriatic. The early risers among the neighborhood elite pretended not to notice as they proceeded with stately self-importance.

One of them bowed obsequiously to Scrovegni. "*Bondì*, Messer Enrico." The Venetian dialect still sounded too soft in the mouth to him; back home on the mainland talk had solid hard edges. Here it was like the houses with showy facades built on stilts in the mud.

"*Bondì*, Messer Paolo." He didn't bother stopping. There was no need for politeness. Paolo Correr owed him money. Rumor had it that pirates off Cyprus had waylaid one of his galleys loaded with spices, silks, and porcelain. That meant Correr would be coming around to ask for an extension. Scrovegni was too tired for his usual quick calculation of how much he would demand.

It was a comfort, even on such a morning, to be in this neighborhood. He had kept enough of his fortune out of the clutches of those predators at home to settle wherever he chose in Venice. As an outsider, he was not bound to some soggy family turf. He had good reasons for deciding on San Maurizio's Contrada, "country" as Venetians grandly called their neighborhoods. It was only a few turns away from the Piazza of San Marco where the Venetians paraded in their glory—never mind that they had to steal their patron saint's remains from Alexandria in Egypt. Maurizio himself was said to have passed from Egypt through the lagoon on his hero's way to martyrdom. His sword from Thebes was a counterpart to the pen of Mark's gospel from Alexandria.

Scrovegni had been devoted to the warrior saint since going to Milan for the crowning of another of those pale northerners with fantasies of empire and order in Italy. Maurizio was the Egyptian commander the Roman emperors had called north to suppress a rebellion; he was put to death with his African legion when they refused to worship the pagan gods or fight the rebels in the Alps who had converted to the True Faith. Maurizio was rewarded many times over as a patron saint of the Christian heirs of the pagan empire. His sword was the coronation sword of the Holy Roman Empire.

"Blessed San Maurizio," the Archbishop of Milan had chanted, "son of Thebes, martyr for the True Faith, patron of soldiers and armies, we ask your protection for this pious Augustus, emperor-elect. Let his strong arm bear your glorious sword to restore peace and justice to this ravaged kingdom of Italy that sheds piteous tears in the hope of deliverance."

When his turn came as Padua's envoy, Scrovegni had stepped forward to kiss the hilt of saint's sword engraved with the imperial eagle. Instead of metal cool to his lips he felt a strange surging warmth. That night a figure radiant in golden armor with an upraised sword of flashing silver appeared to him in a vision or a dream—he was not sure which. He shielded his eyes against a blinding light. "Honor me," a voice called out and then in an unintelligible tongue issued what sounded like another command. The voice trailed off and the figure vanished into the black emptiness of sleep.

Scrovegni often pondered that apparition of Maurizio, if that is what it was. The command came back to him, especially in times of danger. He had played the game of advance, feint, and retreat in Padua, knowing all the while that everything could be lost with a wrong move. The city and its territory were coveted by latest strongmen or warlords acting on behalf of some emperor or a pope, or claiming to do so. One of many quick shifts in allegiances led to his flight into exile. Fair-weather friends called him a coward, but no one could call him a fool, and it would have been foolish to stay in Padua.

But it was not his way to be without defenses. The emperor, Henry VII, he saw crowned as King of the Romans in Milan, was laid low by the most reliable Italian defenses, treachery and fever. There was a scramble of rivals after his death. Scrovegni was prepared to offer the winner a wondrous gift. A precious image of the patron saint of the Holy Roman Empire. What wouldn't an emperor-in-waiting give for this sign of his legitimacy? And how could such an offering—and a pledge of generous credit—fail to bring about Scrovegni's return in triumph to Padua?

Now, years later, Scrovegni was resigned to triumphing in absentia, in the Arena church. The order of things was complete and perfect there. In the imperfect world he had found another use for the gift he had intended for an emperor; it hung in the saint's Venetian church as a testimony to his devotion to San Maurizio and as an offering to his Venetian neighbors, who doubted that any outsider was worthy to live among them.

Lionardo escorted Scrovegni to his pew at the front of San Maurizio's church and helped him rise as the priest began: "In the name of the Father, the Son, and the Holy Spirit. I shall go to the altar of God who giveth joy and the holy martyr Maurizio whose sword of indomitable faith promises strength in this world…"

***

Regina's expedition to Padua kept coming back to her all week. She decided she had to follow up on the half-joking, half-serious title about the

Arena chapel as Enrico Scrovegni's "best deal." Searching on line, she saw that there was a copy of the book in the Biblioteca Marciana. The library was open on Saturday mornings, so she could go from there to meet Flavia at their yoga class in nearby Campo San Maurizio.

The Marciana was a favorite place of hers, a hidden treasure in plain sight across from the Doge's Palace in the dogleg *piazzetta*, the little piazza off Piazza San Marco. Not quite in plain sight, she had to admit as she came to the dingy entrance of the working library. The library's showpiece Renaissance gallery was upstairs, annexed to the Correr Museum with its own entrance. Down below, between glitzy shops crowding in contemptuously on both sides, a heavy pair of recessed doors was guarded by muscle-bound marble statues that looked like bouncers; braving their scowls and clenched fists, you came to a booth on the inside resembling a sentry box.

That had taken some getting used to. But Regina was comfortable by now with the Marciana as a refuge for readers that libraries were supposed to be. It was the oldest public library anywhere. The magnificent colonnaded reading room was once the courtyard of the mint. A perfect Venetian combination. Money consorting with high culture, an investment in learning, time travel, and books you didn't know you wanted to read.

After passing the credentials check, she went to the circulation counter to submit her requests. In the Marciana that meant filling out little paper slips and waiting for shuffling porters to deliver books like the ministers of a sacred order pledged to keep the digital invasion at bay. She did her duty to the Bellini by requesting a 16th-century book by a Venetian humanist scholar who might have known them, but it was the Scrovegni book that she really wanted to see. While waiting at one of the worn oak tables with flickering reading lights, she texted Flavia to confirm their date for lunch after yoga class.

When her books were delivered, the one on the chapel was dauntingly thick but inviting too in a cheery orange binding. The humanist's little treatise would have to wait; he would have been used to that. It was not news that Renaissance art was the patron's deal, plausibly his best one, but leafing through the Scrovegni book, Regina was struck by how the author, Chiara Frugoni, blended close-grained erudition with enchantment. The chapel was no less dazzling, maybe even more so, as a transaction between Scrovegni's self-interest, Giotto's painting, and the susceptibilities of viewers past and present.

The book quoted from Scrovegni's will as a character study of the man. Even in the Latin legalese and the Italian translation of "wheres and wherefores" Regina felt something like the jolt of excitement that had struck her in front of Giotto's Scrovegni portrait:

Imprimis ego Enricus Scrovenus condam Raynaldi Scrovegni civis Padue et Venetiarum eligo mei corporis sepulturam apud ecclesiam et in ecclesia Sancte Marie de Caritate de l'Arena de Padua, scilicet in monumento in ipsa constructo per me...

First of all, I, Enrico Scrovegni, citizen of Padua and of Venice, elect as the burial place for my body the church of Saint Mary of Charity at the Arena of Padua, that is, in the monument constructed there by and for me...

That sounded like the man in Giotto's portrait alright. But "citizen of Padua and *Venice?*" Regina hadn't realized that Scrovegni ever lived anywhere besides his native Padua, much less that he was a citizen of Padua and Venice too.

Thumbing back a few pages, she noticed that the will had been sealed and witnessed at the monastery of San Mattia on the islands of Murano; just offshore from Venice, Murano would have been a suburban retreat for people like Scrovegni. She had made the must-see excursion on the #12 vaporetto to tour the famous glass workshops there. Most souvenir Murano glass probably came from China now, but the tourists didn't know the difference and there wasn't anything anachronistic about the China connection. Marco Polo had voyaged halfway around the planet to the court of Kublai Khan; no one believed him until he produced some Chinese treasures and even then people joked about Marco of the Million Fibs. He had a belated revenge when historians had come around to admitting that mobility, globalization, and connectivity were not modern—or postmodern—inventions.

But where had Scrovegni lived? The will went on about his property in and around Padua without mentioning Venice. But a footnote in the scholarly introduction cited a document referring to his Venetian residence in the Contrada of San Maurizio. Regina caught her breath, startling the dozing student across from her. The saint's parish church was next to the yoga studio where she was going to meet Flavia in less than an hour.

It hardly seemed possible, the timing or the place. The location was a Venetian rarity—depressing. San Maurizio's Campo, Venetian for "field" and "piazza" in a city short on the real thing, was cramped and dreary. On one side an abandoned school—it must have been a Renaissance palace in better days—glowered toward a row of anonymous brick buildings, most of them with peeling doors and clusters of corroded nameplates.

The namesake church was angled off-center, with a sterile white façade that looked like it had been glued onto a new building in the 19th century. The imitation classical replacement that must have been the height of fashion in the 1820s had turned into another of those sad rejects converted into warehouses, performance spaces, or galleries of schlock art. Sounds of recorded Vivaldi wafted out of San Maurizio at all hours from someone's vanity collection of stringed instruments. Marcella's yoga studio was on a third, low rent floor above a Catholic charity association and a dentist's office.

Regina stayed at the Marciana taking notes until the noon closing time. Yoga class had already started before she could join in. *Abitiamo al sospiro e sentiamo la pace dell'universo intero*, the middle-aged yoga teacher intoned. "Let us inhabit the breath and feel the peace of the universe." It was going to be hard to concentrate, but Regina stretched into the pigeon pose and tuned out what her teacher was saying. New Age babble sounded just as silly to her in Italian as it did in English. She did yoga for the exercise, not to find the pathway to enlightenment.

She just went through the motions this time. She was impatient to head out with Flavia after class. "Marcella's good," Flavia said as they went down the grimy stairs. "I just wish she'd cut out that Ram Krishna bullshit. It gives me a headache."

"Just wait till you hear what's buzzing around in my head."

They found a table at Le Café in nearby Campo Santo Stefano. The waiter took their order for a prosecco and some cicchetti, little open-faced sandwiches of deviled shrimp, anchovies and mayonnaise, and roast pork with arugula.

"The Scrovegni was fantastic," Regina began.

Flavia rolled her eyes. "This is a surprise? Maybe for you Americans."

Regina was used to Flavia's teasing, but she had a come-back this time. "Well, how about this? I've been reading about Scrovegni at the Marciana. It turns out that he lived somewhere right around here. He never got back to Padua. Died in Venice."

"So Marcella could channel him?"

"*Basta, Flavia.* I looked up Maurizio just before coming to class. I didn't have much time, but I found out he wasn't the saint you'd expect from the name of a posh Swiss resort town. He was Egyptian, commander of a Roman legion, ordered to put down a revolt in the Alps. A Christian convert executed with all his men for not fighting rebels who were Christians too. And he was black."

"*Accidenti!* You beat me on surprises this time."

"I don't know. When I was a kid my parents took us on a Mardi Gras vacation trip to New Orleans; we saw a statue of a black Saint Maurice—that's what he's called down there. It was in the black neighborhood that got flooded out by Hurricane Katrina. Anyway, this got me wondering again about the black man in Giotto's flagellation in Padua.

"The only black guy there, handsome too. When I was working over there on the chapel restoration, I thought he seemed to be holding himself apart from the officials on one side and the gang bullying Jesus on the other. Frozen. Even appalled." Flavia grinned. "Maybe Scrovegni had a thing for black guys."

Regina couldn't resist. "Weren't you checking out that African guy in the tour group that just went by?"

"What do you think? It looks like we've both got more research to do."

***

Enrico Scrovegni had not seen Giotto di Bondone since he finished working in the Arena chapel. The painter had left a memento there, a self-portrait among the legions of the saved in the Last Judgment. He stood out as a stubby figure with a big head in a pointed white hat. He had joked with Scrovegni about this. "Consider this, Messer Enrico. Such an ugly sinner among those bound for Paradise bears witness to the wondrous effects of your piety."

Since then, Giotto's fame had grown beyond measure from one end of Italy to another. Would he agree to paint again for a former patron without a crown, a cope, or a mitre? Scrovegni would find out. In a letter to Florence, "or wherever the Master might be," he offered a commission for a portrait of San Maurizio.

"You'll have to pay through the nose this time," muttered Ser Rafaino, the household notary who drafted his letters and kept his accounts. He knew that it wouldn't matter when his master had set his mind to something.

Giotto had worked for the Franciscans in many places with as little concern as many of them for the virtues of poverty. He had written a biting poem about the hypocrisy of vows of poverty when there were better uses for wealth. Scrovegni remembered some of its lines:

> *I call it shame and ill*
> *To name a virtue that which stifles still,*
> *To make virtue's advent*
> *on a thing so bestial dependent.*
> *Here, on earth, those who poverty preach*
> *Are those who are in their hypocrisy*
> *Least at peace.*

Scrovegni thought well of the poem, but he was not so pleased to read Giotto making the argument in prose.

20

Most illustrious and honorable Lord, greetings from your servant Giotto di Bondone. It would indeed be my honor once more to obey your command. I shall endeavor to do justice to the trust you have bestowed on me to make a likeness as you desire of the blessed San Maurizio executed by my own hand and none other. In keeping with the virtue of magnanimity for which you are everywhere known, you will no doubt agree to reward my humble work beyond the generous offer you have tendered.

A strange world this, where a painter, even Giotto, could set his own terms. But Scrovegni was determined to have this painting and certain that it would be worth the price.

He remembered Maurizio coming up between Giotto and Dante in one of those verbal bouts the Florentines like so much. That was when the scribbler came to Padua to visit his friend of better days; before, as Dante told it to those who would listen and many who would not, the mongrel race of ingrates in Florence had driven him to eat strangers' salty bread in exile. Scrovegni, eating the Venetians' bread, knew what he meant.

Gesturing toward the newly painted walls in the Arena church, Dante had launched into what must have been an old argument with Giotto. "I admit," he began, "that this is an improvement on the mess of plaster you started with. But they're still only mute things for all that."

"So you say it's better to tell with a scratchy quill what my brush can show in an instant. Without needing a pagan poet and a dead maiden muse, your Virgil and Beatrice, to guide my hand."

"You expect praise, *caro mio*? Not the contempt you deserve for forgetting the lowly place your filthy smock and stained hands ought to remind you of?"

Giotto glanced with mock surprise at Dante's hands. "And the ink on yours? When my figures do with a gesture, a look, what you need black-scrawled lines for, and at the end are nothing more than words."

"Ah, the delightful simplicity of the artisan"—Dante was prepared for the insult—"who only copies at a distance what God has made and shamelessly claims it as the product of his vainglorious judgment and feeble intellect."

"So God did not give us sight and things to behold for good reason? To marvel in the wonders of his creation?" Giotto pointed at the figure of the blackamoor on the south wall. "Those we know and those that are singular and unexpected."

"You mean the one who looks ready to strike our Lord? Or is that what he is doing? You have placed him between the mocking brutes and the scheming priests behind him. We don't know how he will act next without words to tell us. He could be an executioner or an Ethiopian with a noble heart who only bad Christians could condemn. So much for your truth in painting."

"Indeed," Giotto replied quietly. "His weapons might be raised for evil or good."

Scrovegni thought Giotto had won the argument. Lionardo was Giotto's model for the Moor in that scene and he had captured the man not just a mask. You could see such a figure raising his weapon as well against evil as for it. Perhaps even as San Maurizio.

The contract he sent back to Giotto was as specific in its conditions as in his other business dealings.

> *The painter Giotto di Bondone will deliver a true likeness of the blessed San Maurizio. The panel is to be made of seasoned wood of fine grain, with no less than one half ounce of gold leaf and the highest quality available hematite and rich colors in every degree of finish. The saint shall be painted in a standing position, in his armor, with his companions, and the finished panel shall be 2 braccia high by 1.5 braccia wide. The figure of the saint must be painted by Giotto di Bondone himself, and not worked upon by anyone else in his workshop. The painter shall receive 150 grossi of silver upon delivery of the completed work.*

The terms of the contract had been met. The painting hung in the church of San Maurizio where Scrovegni was accustomed to kneel, his hands crossed in prayer, craving the surge of power he had once felt on touching the saint's sword in Milan. He could not be sure how much longer his body would obey. The final disposition of the likeness of San Maurizio had been left unresolved in his will. He would have to provide for it in perpetuity as one more proof of his faith, hope, and charity just in case any further proof were needed.

***

Regina had ordered two *pezzi*, "pieces" in archive slang, to be held for her at the Archivio di Stato. She had begun to learn her way around the Mother Church of historians as someone had called that monument to Venice's many centuries of scribes, notaries, and secretaries. It was funny to think of it that way. It sat unassumingly, almost anonymously, on the cloister side of the great church that the Franciscans, *Frari* in Venetian dialect, had stocked with priceless masterpieces while preaching poverty. As for the Bellini, the archive had not been nurturing. *Some mother*, Regina thought.

It was all very well to talk the new art-history-speak about transnationalism, hybridization, and deconstruction. Not that Regina believed people always knew what they were talking about with those terms. She was quite sure, however, that the hard thing for historians of Renaissance art, especially early Renaissance art, was finding much evidence in the archives or anywhere else. Giotto was an archival blank; a century or more later the Bellini achieved semi-noble status, but records about them were few and far between even in the age of virtuoso celebrities like Leonardo and Michelangelo. The archive was the proverbial haystack where you hoped to find the needle by shuffling through old papers. At least Regina knew where Scrovegni's will was thanks to her Marciana reading. She decided to page the original and to look for materials from the neighborhood where he had lived.

As it had turned out, there didn't seem to be much about the Contrada of San Maurizio. Or so she had surmised from a morning's search. While you could request documents at prescribed hours by computer, the routines of an archival Twilight Zone episode had not come very far into the digital age. Not many documents had been scanned and just finding the call numbers of a documentary series was not easy. You might find them, or not, in long rows of bound inventories containing blurry photocopies of earlier inventories with generations of inked-in corrections in the margins.

On her way out for lunch Regina had stopped to ask Dottoressa Zanardi for advice. Zanardi was one of the senior archivists who took turns at the main desk. She had signed Regina into the Archivio without bureaucratic folderol on her first day. Archivists knew more about the collections than anyone else, but some scholars were too awkward to ask for help or too self-important to think of archivists as much more than plumbers or failed historians. Zanardi was congenial and helpful from the beginning. When Regina asked about the original of Scrovegni's will, she checked the call number in Regina's notes and nodded that it was indeed in the archives of the Procurators of San Marco, the officials who reviewed legacies and bequests.

"Three copies of it. It's a good thing too. You'll see when you look at them." Zanardi was not at all optimistic about materials for the Contrada of San Maurizio. "Difficult, I'm afraid. So much was lost there. But you might search in this." She wrote down the name of an archival series Regina wouldn't have known to search in for her archival needle. Zanardi went over to the shelf of inventories. "Alvise is at the counter this afternoon and he'll order the Scrovegni file and this for you"—she handed Regina a slip of paper with unfamiliar call numbers—"if you page them now and come back after lunch."

The Italian custom of a long lunch break used to be inviolable, with time for a sit-down meal back home, a glass of wine, and a good nap or perhaps some love-making. Regina never knew where and when the old rules would be observed. She made do with a short lunch. When she returned her requests were waiting for her on one of those carts the archival staff wheeled around with yellowing paper like jaundiced patients. Thanking Alvise, she had carried her *pezzi* to her desk. The soaring Renaissance colonnade of the Frari's old cloister had long since been converted to secular worship as a reading room for Venetian regulars, visiting scholars, and anxious students bent over their work or spying on what others were doing.

Regina opened a worn file box labeled "Scrovegni." It looked like a reject from an office supply store back home; the makeshift folder inside made of old blotter paper was even more anticlimactic. But she still felt a shiver of anticipation as she opened it carefully to a formal text of the will written in an official-looking hand on parchment. The stately artifact of the notarial profession was torn, faded, and covered in places by some kind of mold that looked like a deep red wine stain. Underneath the parchment original there were two badly damaged copies that were evidently intact in the illegible sections on the original; this was how the whole text had been reconstructed in the appendix to Frugoni's book. The scholarly reconstruction inspired confidence, but Regina savored the time-travel feel of the documents and the sense of Scrovegni's presence. *Another good deal for you that these copies got made, Messer Enrico.* She replaced the pages carefully, compensating for the indignity of their container.

The other *pezzo* was more than a foot thick. Its shabby cardboard covers were tied together by scraps of twine and tape. She couldn't imagine why Zanardi had suggested that she look at it. The contents, according to a note written on the cover, dated from the late 18th century and documented the suppression of religious institutions following Napoleon's dissolution of the once-proud Venetian republic in 1797. Napoleon was still a bogeyman in Venice. Regina remembered reading a newspaper story about costumed judges in powdered wigs convened to try the little Corsican for crimes against civilization. The Napoleonic regime of the short-lived "Kingdom of Italy" had set about inventorying libraries and art works for confiscation, transport to Paris, or outright sale at auction. The official commissioners' records were an unabashed chronicle in thousands of pages of a looting operation.

Untying the covers, she saw that they held a stack of paper folders made of recycled documents and arranged in punctilious alphabetical order. Leafing through the folders, she came near the bottom to one unpromisingly thin folder labeled "S. Maurizio." The first pages were printed excerpts from a decree of 1806 shutting down charitable confraternities, or *scuole* as the Venetians still called them, associated with the church of San Maurizio. There was a list of items scheduled for expropriation: candlesticks, benches, a silk altar cloth, a chalice, a large silver reliquary, pictures in the wooden framing on the ceiling and a few framed pictures, none of them specifically identified, on the walls of the parish house and a meeting room.

Farther on, Regina came to testimony from some parishioners and the records of a dispute between San Maurizio's parish priest, one Antonio Armani, and a pawnbroker by the name of Iseppe Bora Levi. The priest had gone to the Napoleonic commissioners to bring suit against Levi and his men for breaking into the church and the parish house to cart off more than they had bid for. They had gone so far, according to Armani, as to strip the little chapel that the bread-makers' guild had leased from the parish since the 15th century. This looked like the kind of petty complaint that filled archives everywhere, in this case with some archetypal Venetian anti-Semitism in Armani's outrage about the "predations of these sons of Israel."

But then a passage caught Regina's eye in Armani's list of allegedly stolen goods. "*Quadro antico. Pare S. Maur.o. Al posto del las.to Scrov.gni ed eredi.* Regina read the sketchy lines over three or four times, trying to decipher what they meant: "Old picture, evidently San Maurizio. In the place of the bequest of Scrovegni and heirs."

Her mind was racing. The smallest Scrovegni reference would have specialists buzzing. And what if—she hardly dared to imagine it—Scrovegni had commissioned a San Maurizio from Giotto for the Contrada's church? So far as she knew, there was no evidence for such a painting, let alone one by Giotto. It was an in-house joke that the most prolific painter of the period was *Maestro Anonimo*—"Anonymous Master." But if Giotto had done a San Maurizio, what had happened to it? And if he had, could it be that the painting had somehow survived? Finding a Giotto hidden away somewhere would be a huge event in the art world.

Regina spent an hour before closing time going through the rest of the file with a shaky hand, photographing what she found with her little Canon. Levi had not appeared in court as he had been ordered to do on September 5, 1808; he was sentenced in absentia on September 19, 1808. But there was nothing else about the picture or the identity of the artist.

Still a little dazed, Regina threaded her way back home. As soon as she got to her apartment, she went online to check: no San Maurizio was listed among Giotto's known works.

***

Enrico Scrovegni's boatmen helped him into the cabin of his waiting gondola after mass at San Maurizio. From morning prayers to business and his private thoughts the old man prided himself on his regular habits even though his body protested.

It was not far on the tributary Rio San Maurizio to the Grand Canal. The same watery element of spiritual salvation in baptism carried material benefits on the great waterway. Scrovegni had heard the philosophers at the university in Padua talk about water as the element between the earth below and air and fire above. The crystalline spheres beyond the moon were of another substance as suited their higher place. Even after many years in Venice he still felt more at home on the mainland's solid ground. Negotiating distances between the spirit and material things was not a philosopher's problem for him.

His gondola negotiated the curve toward the Rialto bridge into the Grand Canal swarming with craft of every size and shape laden with sacks, barrels, and boxes. The boatmen swerved to miss a little skiff heading back from the markets with bags of live eels and squawking fowls bound for some palace kitchen.

Scrovegni was a force to be reckoned with on the Rialto. It pleased him to show that he was no small town mainland magnate. The Rialto was the world's grandest stage for business. You could buy, trade, or sell anything there: salt from Ibiza and spices from the Levant; pilgrims' robes; lead and alum from the Black Sea; leather from Cordova and Tunis; English wool from London and Southampton; wheat from Sicily and Sardinia; oranges and wine from Syria and Catalonia; white slaves from the Black Sea and black ones from Africa. You did not need to travel the long-distance trading routes across the Mediterranean and beyond on the Silk Road or venture through Gibraltar to bring back English wool. Scrovegni chose instead to collect on his well-placed loans and some inland trade; he left the risks to others. The Polos had made a career out of inviting risks and young Marco had come back from what he said was a fabulous empire in the East with little to show for it.

The gondola pulled up to the moorings by the Rialto bridge. There were no traces left to show that rebels had set fire to it not many years earlier. That was best forgotten. Back in Padua, Scrovegni had spoken up in a council meeting against the Doge and his allies who were hell-bent on lording it over the Republic. He was usually more guarded in his opinions, at least in public, even when provoked time and again. A Venetian spy had reported back what he had said in council, but nothing had come of it. Fortunately. The Venetians were ruthless, for all their fine republican talk. Yes, better to forget and to act the good citizen.

By habit of long standing, Scrovegni made the rounds on the Rialto, attending to his loans, exchanging the latest news, acknowledging real respect and ignoring the other kind. He needed now to show that he was up to managing his own affairs and that he expected to collect what was owed to him.

On this particular morning he was distracted by unfinished business of a kind that could not be dealt with on the Rialto. Loose ends left the future to chance and to those ready to cheat, undercut, outmaneuver you. His papers were stored against such possibilities in the chests at Ca' Scrovegni: account books, inventories, deeds, lists of payments, bills of lading. His most private papers he kept under lock and key in a fine-tooled chased silver box from the Levant.

Among these, tied with a silk ribbon, were his papers concerning San Maurizio, the saint and his church. He had prayed for many years now at San Maurizio's altar, where his promised donation of the saint's portrait had been installed.

"Summon Ser Rafaino to my chambers," he told Lionardo on returning to Ca' Scrovegni from his Rialto rounds. Helped from the gondola, he made his way slowly onto the dock, through the long hall, and up the stairs to his own quarters. He slumped in the chair by the chest guarding his most important papers, then slowly straightened himself to lend proper dignity to the occasion. The notary bowed his way into the room and took his place at the desk in the corner.

"I want you to draw up deeds for the objects I have promised to churches in Venice."

"Which shall I do first, Signore."

"Begin with San Maurizio."

***

What should I tell Terterian? Regina didn't want to think that watching out for herself had to be sneaky or conniving. The discovery was hers, but to call the document hers felt more like a joke than a serious claim. Not to mention the flight of fancy that her find in the archive somehow made her an accomplice with obligations to Scrovegni, and maybe to Giotto.

But what about the Bellini? Terterian had encouraged her Bellini research, leaned on it even. When she got bogged down writing applications for a research grant, he egged her on. "It's is a special genre. Don't worry. It's like learning to ride a bicycle; next time you'll wonder why it took you so long this time."

When the grant came through he had taken her out to celebrate. "It will give me an excuse to come to Venice," he had said. "Only to keep an eye on your progress of course."

Regina was grateful, if sometimes a little regretful too, that Terterian was gay. He was good-looking, with his olive complexion and Roman nose, young enough and well-proportioned enough to carry off his tight jeans and slicked back retro hair. They had tacitly agreed early on that the professional mentor-advisee relationship was not going to be complicated by romance or sex.

The Bellini hadn't lost their charm for Regina. Especially Giovanni's uncanny blend of intimate tenderness, mysterious distance, and the Venetian lagoon greens and atmospheric blues that his turn to painting in oil put before your eyes again and again. On breaks from the archive she liked to go over to the Frari to look at his Madonna and Child. The pompous funeral monuments of a carnival of death around the walls left her cold. But the Bellini picture in the sacristy looked like it had been painted yesterday, not a half a millennium ago. She knew it had been restored, not for the first time either, a few years earlier, but it reminded her that her Bellini project was not just Terterian's idea. To look at their work in light of their family enterprise, their social standing, their connections with the East—Gentile Bellini had served as a court painter of Sultan Mehmet, the Ottoman conqueror of Constantinople—could make their pictures all the more compelling. And it would be in keeping with new directions in art history.

That's not changed, Regina thought. She loved what she had taken to calling B.C.—Bellini Cool. But the chances of tracing their "network," as the newer studies would have it, were slim. *And now that Scrovegni, a black saint, and—don't I wish?—a lost Giotto have come into my life...*

That sounded ridiculous. But she rationalized that scholars probably weren't very serious if they didn't get obsessed. *This art historical mystery triangle of mine,* she told herself, *nothing wrong with a romance like that.*

Besides, the "affair" had begun to look like a "deal"—she liked the Scrovegni riff—with larger stakes than an academic exercise. In the States she got by under a multicultural veneer where race was not supposed to matter much, at least among her friends and colleagues. In Italy she got over being a curiosity, a black person who was neither male nor from Sudan or Somalia. The three big volumes on the *Image of the Black in Western Art* were important to her, but they felt too often—and she was put off by this—like token affirmative action.

The medieval and Renaissance volumes mostly reinforced stereotypes. The black figures, if they weren't downright monstrous, played bit parts in Christian conversion stories as one of the Three Wise Men or the African brides and queens recruited from the Old Testament. The population of black pictorial villains—devils from Hell and Satan himself, Muslim soldiers, freaks on the margins of the old maps—was much larger. But Scrovegni, the Arena, a Giotto San Maurizio. Weren't they acting out a different story? Regina was close to making a vow, a pledge or a wild bet, on the far side of what happens to scholars with an obsession.

That was an excuse—not a very good one, she had to admit—for avoiding a link Terterian had sent her for an article on some recent Bellini family research. *I'm sorry, Professor Terterian, but it's not really what I'm looking for just now.*

After stalling long enough to make her point, she clicked on the link. "Oh my God!" she blurted out. There on the cover of the latest *Renaissance Quarterly* was an elegant drawing inscribed "S. Mauritius." He was wearing fantasy armor in a curvy Renaissance pose. There was a halo around his winged helmet; he wore a sword on his belt; in his right hand he held a spear, in his left a martyr's palm and a shield inscribed "For the Holy Cross." He looked like a paper-doll mix of Roman soldier and Christian crusader. He was white.

Scrolling down quickly, she saw that the image came from a Venetian manuscript attributed to Giovanni Bellini and dated around 1453. That was the year when the Turks finally captured Constantinople. Giovanni Bellini's nephew Gentile (not his brother, according to the *Quarterly* article) had gone to Istanbul and painted a scimitar-sharp profile of Sultan Mehmet the Conqueror. Was Giovanni's martyred warrior saint cued to nostalgia for a lost cause; or to hopes for a new crusade? Regina didn't find any answers in the tightly technical article. She was not going to find out more about San Maurizio there and that was what she really wanted to know. She was hooked.

She had already followed some leads in the web's maze of false starts and invented facts. Except for true believers, the look of saints changed or got mixed up over time. The black saint could turn white and probably black again. Who knew what San Maurizio looked like anyway? He had his devotees and hadn't been de-sainted—Regina wondered whether there was such a word—like poor St. Christopher, but it was quite possible that he didn't exist outside pious legends and the prayers of the faithful.

One click brought up his sword as an identifying sign, another his spear. Sometimes one was identified as the other; different swords and spears were supposed to be authentic, none of them convincingly. The rival claims were all the more intense for having very little evidence to back them up. A warrior-saint probably carried a sword and a spear, and other weapons besides. *At least there's only one Shroud of Turin,* Regina muttered.

But San Maurizio had already rattled her doubts about miracles. It was a little miraculous, an eerie coincidence anyway, to discover that the oldest known version of the sword and a still older version of the spear actually existed and had ended up in one and the same place. Both were in the treasure collection of the Habsburg emperors in Vienna. So far as she could tell, they got there at different times through a heavy fog of disappearances, recoveries, and wishful thinking.

Terterian always said that you needed to look for yourself. He didn't mean looking at relics and imperial regalia, but Regina was going to take him at his word. Even though she didn't have much reason to suppose that she could find out much more in Vienna, she had given up thinking that reason had much to do with what she was looking for.

***

"Last time I saw him here old Scrovegni already had one foot in the grave," said Jacopo Gradenigo over a glass of Malvasia at the end of the day on the Rialto. Rumors travel faster in Venice than gondolas or galleys and it didn't cost anything to launch them. A rich man's death was always fair sailing for gossip. The Ca' Scrovegni was still draped in black velvet months after its master's demise. Death in Venice, like everything else there, was an elaborate production if you could afford it. Enrico Scrovegni's heirs certainly could.

Giovanni Marcello laughed. "Must not have been taking enough of that witch's brew from the Giudecca that's supposed to cure all your ailments. Or not loading enough prayers and gifts on San Maurizio."

"He did put on a good face, though, like he always did," Gradenigo admitted. "Ready to do business right to the end. Ser Rafaino is still going around collecting on his loans."

Giovanni Marcello flashed a knowing grin. "So you and your brother just had your run-in with Ser Rafaino's little account book."

"Maybe so, just like you and Andrellino, I'll wager."

Marcello shrugged. "What's to expect with a Marchese's daughter to provide for? Everybody knows the widow was unhappy with what she got. She petitioned to get back her dowry price. I don't know why the Procurators in charge of these things gave her what she wanted. The only dowry she brought to old Scrovegni was a fancy family name. He was within his rights to leave Madonna Jacopina just her clothes, her jewels…"

"And his bed!" roared Andrellino Marcello. "She'll satisfy herself soon enough with some young blood to lie in it."

The conversation halted while another flask of wine was fetched. The sun had just begun to set and the benches, the *banchi* where business got done, were being stowed away. The market people had already packed their wares away for another day.

After another round or two of Malvasia, Bellotto Gradenigo warmed up to the old man. "Well, he was a shrewd old bugger, but you can't say that he was a cheapskate like so many old farts holding out until the devil takes them. A Marchese's daughter from Ferrara for a wife, dowries big enough for his girls to marry high up, a couple of young sons coming on— all that cost him many a ducat."

Bellotto's brother Jacopo chimed in. "And in Padua, living like a prince. Spent a fortune at the Arena, and it cost him a treasure of grief too. The Carrara and their toughs could hardly wait to take over everything. His place here in San Maurizio is grand enough but nothing like what he had to leave."

"You don't hear the priests complaining about his being stingy," Bellotto added.

Giovanni Marcello grinned. "Or the money-making they preach against. When they're in the pulpit. Where would they be without us poor sinners? I heard that the priest over at San Samuele pawned the church silver and an ebony crucifix with Scrovegni; the fool could have got what he wanted for nothing if he said it was for the good of the soul. How much do you think your soul is worth, Messer Bellotto?"

There was a loud guffaw from the rest of the company; accounts for their souls weren't being questioned. "Anyway," Bellotto went on, "Messer Enrico wasn't just beholden to his account books or whatever the priests told him. You're not going to see money bags in that likeness of him in his chapel. He's at the head of the saved ones, body and soul, in the Last Judgment; he's leaving the priest to do the heavy lifting of the model church he's presenting to the Virgin. They look like they're having a private chat, the Virgin and Scrovegni; the priest's just keeping his mouth shut beneath them."

"There's money bags there alright, *Bellotto mio*. Hanging around the necks of Judas and the usurers with their guts spilling out. One of them has got the Scrovegni sow figured on his purse.

Marcello went on. "And what about Dante insulting old Raynaldo Scrovegni as a raging moneylender in that so-called *Commedia* of his? A fine reward for getting himself invited to Padua when Giotto was working for Messer Enrico. I wouldn't put it past the scribbler, finding fault or making it up. That's a Florentine for you. But it doesn't matter. Pictures and scribbling don't matter much in the grave."

"But look here, Giovanni, what matters is that Messer Enrico's out in front. He's himself in the picture, only finer there. Ransoming his soul for the resurrection and his family's too."

Marcello shrugged. "In the picture, you say. If it doesn't turn out that way, no one will be the wiser until it really happens."

"Well, Scrovegni and Giotto were in their prime back then, outdoing everybody, even the old Romans."

"Hear, hear, Bellotto. You'll be wanting me to believe next that Messer Enrico is telling the Virgin the stories on the walls. One thing's sure; the heirs are not likely to get back to Padua very soon to hear him. Those Carrara lords, as they call themselves, will see to that."

The bells at San Giacomo had begun to ring for evening mass. "Anyway this flask's empty. Let's go on to Bepi's place while our women pray for us in church."

***

To Marsiglio Carrara, Illustrious Lord of the City and Commune of Padua and our Captain General, Felicitous Greetings, etc.

Pursuant to the oath of Your Magnificence on the sixth day of the present month to restore peace and prosperity to the City and Commune of Padua we commend to you the last will and testament of the noble lord and knight Enrico Scrovegni, deceased 22 August 1336 in Contrada San Maurizio of this Most Serene Republic, whereby his body is to be transferred for burial in the church he has erected and ornamented, namely, S. Maria della Carità dell'Arena. The said deceased has further stipulated that certain payments be made on his account from properties in the dominion of said City and Commune of Padua. Wherefore, with the filial respect and obedience due to their late father, his sons Bartolomeo and Ugolino degli Scrovegni wish to present themselves before your Magnificence to seek your good offices in settling their father's estate. As co-executors for the estate of said Lord Enrico we ask that Your Magnificence look favorably on their petition to fulfill the last wishes of your fellow citizen and, by decree of the Senate, citizen of this Most Serene Republic.

In the Palace of the Procurators of S. Marco, 18 August 1337, Giustiniano Giustiniani and Francesco Contarini, Procurators

~

To the Magnificent Lords Procurators of S. Marco, Greetings as Reverend Fathers, etc.

We are in receipt of your missive with respect to our erstwhile citizen Enrico Scrovegni. While obliged to honor and observe your just petitions, we must remind your Excellencies of the long history of slight and deceit of said deceased. He last appeared in this noble city nine years ago by cover of night bearing gifts of golden rings and pearls to the invading tyrant of Verona, Cangrande della Scala. He had abandoned our noble city in its hour of great need some years previously. His professions of friendship and allegiance were betrayed by the treachery of his nephews Gabardo and Romaldo and the unpaid dowry owed to me in marriage with his niece, a barren wife. Against these injuries and onerous debts we justly confiscated the properties of said deceased in this Noble City and its territories, wherefore his minor sons and other would-be creditors have no legitimate claims. Therefore we must reject his directives to our dishonor and our expense with the firmness and resolve they deserve and, accordingly, we shall not permit his body to return to defile this Noble City.

Marsilius de Carrensibus, Lord of the City and Commune of Padua and Captain General, etc.

2

Duccio Chiarini didn't care for art dealers. Pompeo Zorzi's "Villa Maravegie" address suggested a Venetian aristocrat's country estate or maybe a magician's hideaway. The name was dialect for marvels or even miracles; Zorzi's rented rooms were neither one nor the other. The flaking faux Renaissance courtyard did little to disguise the sagging palazzo on a narrow Dorsoduro canal. Zorzi talked like the rest of his kind about his table at Florian's, the box at La Fenice, the grand hotels on the Riva degli Schiavoni and the Lido. He wasn't lying all the time. That's where the dealers' hunting grounds were.

There was always a reliable market for scenes of Venice, bad or indifferent souvenirs of the Grand Tour or the economical Baedeker trip. Chiarini had little use for strutting foreigners in the galleries saying stupid things about those "impressions," as they called *vedute* of Venice now. He was Tuscan, old school, proud of it. Pigments drowned in oil had made painting too easy, not to mention watercolor that you splashed on paper in no time at all. The craft of gold leaf, tempera, and fresco, the meticulous care of the old masters, had been all but lost. Not altogether, though; not in Siena and not in his own studio.

The manservant in white jacket and striped waistcoat showed him into a sitting room with marble niches and walls covered in champagne-colored silk. Two matching chests with grinning Bombay fronts stood on either side of the fireplace with a mantel of vaguely classical reliefs. A halo of paintings and prints hung above polished mahogany curves, damask cushions, a Turkish brass table top on an ebony tripod, spiraling Murano glass. The display was staged to show that good taste could be bought with the advice of the master of the house.

Zorzi made his entrance in a violet smoking jacket and carpet slippers. "Ah, *caro Chiarini*, not everyone has forgotten old friends in these dark days." Did he mean his visitor or himself? Chiarini had no doubt when Zorzi sat down first before offering him a chair and launched into his overture.

"You were not here of course when the Austrians bombed night after night in '17. A sacrilege! For what? A Cheating Peace. Robbed to make a paper state of Slavs with nothing in common but hating one another. Then the Crash, '29—*miseria*! And now this thirteenth year of the Duce. Not a lucky number. Sanctions from those self-appointed guardians of political morality for taking our just retribution in Africa. This brotherhood of thieves calling itself a League of Nations. *Ahimè!* So many hypocrites, so many new Philistines. The innocent Madonnas, the dear sweet angels, the solemn saints, the colors, the gold—only a dead past, they say, no future there. No wonder the English milords and uncouth Americans needing our civility don't come for the season anymore."

Chiarini listened to the monologue in silence. He didn't say that he was on the front fighting the Austrians in 1917. Or that he had marched against the Fascists in Siena. "Fewer outsiders to look down their noses at us," he finally mumbled. "Telling me how paintings are made when they don't know how to hold a brush." Then, more quietly, "But you don't know that either, *caro Signore.*"

Zorzi went on. "But we must admit that there are some benefits. No harm done if old families turn needy, as they always do, and sell a few pieces when they still have whole galleries full. Or when a priest wants to get rid of pictures stacked away to rot in the dark corners of his church. Why not turn a town hall's crumbling artifacts to good account? Make the greedy Jews disgorge the treasures pawned with them. For collectors and museums to delight in—and pay for. And what about you, *caro Chiarini?* You have done your patriotic duty, shall we say, in making the most of your old Tuscan masters."

Chiarini waited to see where this was going.

"To adapt but to fulfill a glorious past, even to perfect it. Is this not the mission of our New Italy? Look at Venice now. The lion of San Marco and the Fasces joined; new celebrations bringing life to the old ones; fresh blood coursing in the veins of the old families. Let the moderns show their tawdry fare at the Biennale and then be gone. Our Old Masters are for the ages. In our small way we must do our part."

Zorzi rose to signal that it was time for business. He glided across the Persian carpet to an easel in the corner. Pivoting, he pulled a green velvet cover away from a wooden panel the color of smoke. It was pieced together out of four strips of different widths, apparently cut from the same wood. The seams were clearly visible but, supported by wooden braces, the panel was apparently intact except for burn marks and water-stains on the surface and a scatter of worm holes and chips at the edges.

"So, *caro mio,* only an old master and the toll of time have worked here, wouldn't you say?

Chiarini glanced at the dealer before turning to the panel. "Poplar. The old painters, many of them, preferred it. Softer than limewood, firmer than willow, easier to work. Strong enough resist the elements, this one."

"I'm certain you mean old, very old. Of the Trecento."

Zorzi turned the panel over without waiting for a response. Lifting it from the stand, he held it up to the light, tipping it from side to side as if conjuring forms from its mottled surface.

"A stunning revelation!" he exclaimed. "In the manner of Giotto; dare I say, from the hand of the master himself. A figure in armor, assured, formidable. A warrior saint, miracle-working. Still capable of working miracles, *caro Chiarini*. If properly treated."

Zorzi finally paused. "Yes. To bring about once again, even in these times, the miracle of rebirth that Giotto himself first brought to the art of painting. Surely you will let the master's legacy and your duty guide you."

***

It was a relief to be back in Siena. All that Venice water and damp didn't sit well with Chiarini. The stony dry hills had their drawbacks, but they were familiar and he suffered them with stolid Tuscan forbearance.

Too much water in one place, too little in the other, he thought as his bus went through Porta Camollia. *That's Italy, too much or too little. The politics up there are all wet. That Zorzi is probably no worse than the rest of them, just looking out for himself. Not that we're taking any prizes with a Fascist mayor and blackshirt squads— and me, the old socialist, keeping my mouth shut.*

He reached over to touch the carefully wrapped package on the seat next to him. The people who wanted pictures made for them in the old days weren't saints; that's why they had saints painted for them. A bribe, a ticket to Paradise, a power play, a thing of beauty, all in one. Sometimes, close at work, he sensed the desire invested in those mute things, especially when they seemed to call out for his care.

Over a glass or two of Chianti with friends he had been known to say that beauty didn't need beautiful bedfellows, and didn't get them very often either. This invited the usual comebacks. "It's a lucky thing for you…." Or "You should know, Duccio." He didn't mind the fun so long as he could be as sure of his craft as the old Siena masters had been. And, he had to admit, even the old Florentine painters were.

So, what about this panel? Zorzi says there's a warrior saint on it. By Giotto. Or in the manner of Giotto. Chiarini smiles at this way of putting it. Manner of? That's a little looser than follower; easier than workshop of. Follower doesn't tell you when; workshop doesn't tell you how much the master had to do with it. From the hand of Giotto? It could be any one of those. Hard to say in its present state.

Stepping off the bus with the package carefully tucked next to his travel case, Chiarini made his way up the hill to his house. He had decided what to write to Zorzi.

36

***

Vicolo de' Pittori
Contrada dell'Oca
Siena

16 April 1935
Egregio Signor Zorzi,

I write to advise you that I have returned to Siena with the object entrusted to my care at Villa Maravegie. You may be certain that it will be secure in my studio and protected there from prying eyes and wagging tongues. Our small hills are the Himalayas of rumor and gossip.
Time will be required to study the object carefully. One must not be in a hurry with such things. They protest against too much haste and too little understanding. They must be coaxed to reveal themselves, as if by a masterful lover.
It is enough for now to confirm that the object is a suffering witness to a long life, bearing as it does the wear and wounds of time. Beyond that, I trust you will be patient while I consider how best to proceed.

In fede,
Duccio Chiarini

~

Villa le Maravegie
Campo S. Trovaso
Venezia

21 April 1935, Anno XIII

Caro Chiarini,

I eagerly await further news of the object in question. Yes, we must keep the details to ourselves lest the harpies of suspicion and jealousy descend from those Himalayas of yours.
I remind you, however, that a lover may succeed by acting forcefully, without hesitation. We can be confident in the outcome, can we not? My confidence is such that I have approached, ever so discreetly, the agent of a certain party who is intent on finding an object of this kind.

My friend has not revealed the identity of his client, but he assures me that this person will spare no effort or expense to obtain a correct image of the warrior martyr Maurizio painted by our greatest of early masters. I urge you to seize this opportunity. To work then, caro Chiarini. This is no time for hesitation.

Zorzi

~

Vicolo de' Pittori
Contrada dell'Oca
Siena

1 May 1935

Egregio Signor Zorzi,

You may be sure that I have given the object my full attention since receiving yours of 21 April. No suitor could be more zealous or attentive to the need for ardor as well as respect. Too much of one and you will have obscured what should be revealed; too much of the other and you will have revealed obscurity. Where to enhance, where to withhold? Respect and mastery. That is always the issue in life as in art.

In fede,
Duccio Chiarini

~

Villa le Maravegie
Campo S. Trovaso
Venezia

15 May 1935, anno XIII

Chiarini,

You must understand that the client of my friend can no longer be put off with promises. One can do that with English and American collectors; they are grasping but foolish and more naive than they think they are.

However, this client has communicated his impatience, indeed displeasure, with Teutonic firmness. If we have an image of San Maurizio reasonably attributed to Giotto, as I have taken the liberty to suggest, he fully expects that the great original among artists will challenge and correct the misrepresentations of a deplorable tradition.

No commander of a Roman legion, he insists, could have been a black Egyptian. The Latin "Maurus" for "black" refers to his dark rage toward sin. The black knight in chain armor in the cathedral of Magdeburg? The credulous Middle Ages took that sculpture to be the saint, but it obviously represents one of his Egyptian soldiers. At least he admits that the brilliance of a national vision failed the great painters in the Age of Dürer when they followed the unfortunate precedent.

I spare you the sour jokes of our German friend about naming a black Ethiopian of the miserable race we have just conquered a patron saint of the German emperors.

An ugly business, Chiarini.

Zorzi

~

Vicolo de' Pittori
Contrada dell'Oca
Siena

17 May 1935

Egregio Signor Zorzi,

Let us match the learned Teutons in their erudition. If the saint has been a chameleon through the ages, he must not mind existing in one color or the other. As I remember from old Professor Tozzi's Latin lessons in school, the Latin "invenire" may just as well mean "find" as "invent." I swear by San Maurizio that I shall find the result that suits him.

In fede,
Chiarini

3

"Looks like your saint is calling you," Flavia said when Regina told her about Maurizio's relics in Vienna. "If you go by train, you can see whether those dreamy Bellini mountains you like so much really are blue."

"But it's hours away."

"Just go. Real Venetians wouldn't think twice about getting away when things are too beautiful here or too hot."

Regina wasn't quite ready to confess that the trip would partly be about getting away from the Bellini project. She had decided to wait until she knew more before filling in Terterian. Maybe Vienna would help. Besides, she could stay with her friend Ayse Arikan there; Ayse had emailed to say she would meet her at the Südbahnhof station.

So it was settled. She would sit back and enjoy the trip. She could have seen the Alps on a clear day from Venice, best of all from the Campanile, but she never wanted to deal with the crowd, the chatter, the mugging for cameras. And even on the clearest days she wouldn't have seen the Alpine roll-out unfolding past her window now. Meadows up to forest and down into deep valleys topped by craggy processionals. Many curves and tunnel blackouts too. *Like my life just now,* she thought. As for the mountains, they really were blue, blue-gray anyway.

And staying in Venice, she wouldn't have been sitting across from the interesting looking guy who got on the train at the Verona stop. North African or maybe Turkish, she guessed. Not a fashion-plate type but handsome, intriguing. His black hair was cut short on the sides and brushed back on top; his skin was an indeterminate brown, neither dark nor light, his face slightly pockmarked; his dark eyes were steady and searching at the same time. Moving easily, even gracefully, he smiled a slightly lopsided smile and asked in a surprisingly soft voice whether Regina would mind if he stowed his bag on the overhead rack above her. Across the aisle the three-year old with a flustered grandmother stopped whining to watch. A pair of gangly blond backpackers who had been staring looked away in embarrassment.

The protocol was not much different on American trains. A perfunctory nod, maybe a hello. "You can put your bag on top if you like," Regina answered. "I'm not getting off until Vienna." Protocol meant missing things you wanted to know and she was curious about the new passenger.

"On top then," he said, lifting the bag above her in an easy gesture. Settling into the seat, he smiled that peculiar smile and looked at her more closely than she would have expected, not to mention the correct protocol. "I'll be getting off first, in Bolzano; just an hour or so away. I'm on a time-out from flying and I like to see the mountains when I can."

Regina followed his gaze toward the window. "I've never seen these mountains *except* by plane."

"But you can't really see them from so high up, you know. I grew up in the mountains not far from here."

"I saw my first real mountain when I was ten."

"In the States? Your Italian is so good."

Italians were given to flattering foreigners who didn't know much Italian or just pretended. The condescension was usually misinterpreted as a compliment. "If only, but thank you," Regina said with a look meant to show she was ahead of the game. "My friends don't complain." She added, "And I need it for my work."

"Which is?"

Regina had practically invited the question. She wished she hadn't. She didn't have a real job. "Research in Venice" sounded too self-important. She made do with bullet points: studying art history; in Venice; in the Renaissance.

She was more than a little surprised that he seemed interested. "So you probably know the town where I grew up. The name of it anyway. Pieve di Cadore."

"Where Titian was born? That's amazing!"

"My mother came from Pieve; met my father when she was a nurse in Libya and brought me back home when he died in the troubles there. But talk about amazing." She couldn't tell whether he meant to be playful or serious. "I wouldn't have guessed you know all about old pictures."

Regina smiled at the hyperbole but mostly with embarrassment about how they had jumped to conclusions. He hardly looked like someone from the Dolomites; he probably didn't believe a black American, a woman even, could be studying Renaissance painting in Venice. Stereotypes didn't fit either one of them. They would both know about appearances being deceiving, but they were falling into identity traps.

She kept it light. "Well, I don't know all about pictures." But then went on to volunteer more than she needed to. "Right now I'd be happy just to find out something about one of them in Vienna. It probably sounds like a joke, but I'm going to look at the treasure collection in the old imperial palace."

"Sounds pretty important to me."

"Probably a wild goose chase."

"Like 'catching flies' in Italian. Well, you never know. There are lots of misses in my business; that makes it better when you're right on target." He didn't explain; the train was already slowing down for the Bolzano station and he got up to take his bag.

"Here's where I get off." He handed her a card. "I live in Milan, but I come to Venice every once in a while; we should get better acquainted, don't you think?" Regina fished in her purse for her own card, still a necessary accessory in Italy.

The Bolzano stop had come much sooner than she wished.

***

Stepping off the train in the Südbahnhof, Regina spotted Ayse and rushed to hug her. "You're an angel. You really didn't need to come, you know."

"It's not that I have more important things to do." Regina felt twinges of nostalgia for Ayse's wry good humor. They had shared an apartment, the rent, and sometimes a bed one semester at Duke. It was second nature for the younger generation in the Turkish diaspora to shift between cultures; whip-smart and open to taking take risks, Ayse had found a good fit in American-style cultural anthropology at Duke. Her dissertation was about sex trafficking between East and West. She had proposed "doing some occasional field work together." Which they had done without letting it become too serious.

Ayse took Regina's arm as they made their way along the platform through the apologetically democratic station. "Let's catch the U-Bahn. We'll go for coffee. You can tell me what you're really doing here."

The coffee house—one of Ayse's favorites—was a classic Viennese rebuke to fashions of the moment. The clientele was relaxed in the formal setting of glass chandeliers, lace curtains, marble table tops, and red plush but not quite comfortable banquettes. An unhurried waiter in the iconic black waistcoat and white apron brought glasses of cool water on a silver tray. Ayse ordered one of the house specials for them both. "My ancestors had to settle for addicting Vienna to coffee when they couldn't conquer it," she said when the waiter brought their *Biedermeyer mit Schlagobers*. "The liqueur and whipped cream on top are the decadent Vienna touch."

Regina hadn't gone into any detail with Ayse about why she was there. She wasn't in a hurry now. Not before catching up—she hadn't seen Ayse since that year in Durham—but also because she wasn't sure what, if anything, she expected to find out in Vienna. Not that she needed excuses for being there. Venice and Vienna had competed for ages in collecting art by fraud or force. There was no love lost between them, especially after the Austrians took over Venice from Napoleon and nearly did so again by invasion in the First World War. Regina felt for the Venetians just listening to the German.

"I suppose you'll be going to look at Italian pictures the Austrians hauled over the Alps," Ayse said during a break in the gossip about old friends and new ones.

Regina was tempted to leave it at that. A "research mission" would sound far-fetched, pretentious too. "Yes, the museums." She hesitated. "But I've got a hunch about some things in the old imperial treasury in the Habsburg palace. Relics of a third-century Christian martyr the emperors called from Egypt to put down an uprising in the Alps: Maurizio, Maurice in French, Moritz up here. They executed him with his soldiers when they refused to worship the emperor's gods and the rebels turned out to be fellow Christians."

"What's so special? I mean there must be other lots of other martyr stories like that."

"Yes, but the thing is he was black, maybe even the first black saint. Except that he sometimes got painted white."

"A shifter, you mean." Ayse laughed. "Like us. A Muslim girl from Turkey doing the anthropology of sex; a black woman from Georgia obsessing about old white guys' art." She reached her hand across the table. "Sounds like you could use an anthropologist on the case."

"Thank you, Dr. Arikan." Regina shook the outstretched hand with stagey formality. "But it's really a job for an art historian, for now anyway. Connecting the saint somehow to a lost picture I'd do anything to track down. Seeing his relics probably isn't going to prove much of anything. But seeing is what art historians are supposed to do."

"In the imperial treasury? There's a sign for it in the courtyard beyond the big arch at the Hofburg entrance: *Schatzkammer* in fancy script. I've never gone in though. Too many tourists milling around there looking for the Boys' Choir and the Riding School. I'll show you. It's on my way to the big library in the Hofburg. I've paged a book about those white Circassian sex slaves the old sultans prized so much. No saintliness there, but maybe I'll check for your Moritz in German.

***

It was not true, Regina discovered, that tourists skipped the Schatzkammer. Their Midas-eyes for treasure were reflected in high ticket prices and an elaborate display of expensive trinkets. She bought a guidebook listing 186 "Crown Jewels" and 172 "Ecclesiastical or Spiritual Treasures." The difference wasn't all that clear. One collection wasn't limited to jewels and the other, according to the guidebook, was endowed with a spiritual aura. The chamber of wonders Regina had imagined was disenchanted by rows of old-style display cases and curatorial captions. A large bouquet of jewel-flowers that looked like hard candy was the only indisputable wonder in sight.

It was not true, either, that Maurizio's sword stood out as she had imagined it would. The main exhibit among "Insignia and Regalia of the Holy Roman Empire" was a gloomy fashion show of jeweled gloves, silk shoes, faded dresses, and embroidered girdles. As if the connections were obvious, the ephemera were juxtaposed with a tooth of John the Baptist, splinters from Christ's cradle, and a piece of the Last Supper's tablecloth. The sword was one of three swords lying flat in a glass case off to one side.

The guidebook was not encouraging. "The precise origin of the Sword of Saint Mauritius is lost in the mists of time." There was no inscription on the sword linking it to the saint; its earliest mention in imperial coronation ceremonies dated from the early 14th century. The weapons experts had determined that the blade was medieval—probably 12th century—as was the inscription on the pommel alluding to the divine right of Christian rulers. "Of course one may speculate that the sword was modeled after the Sword of Saint Mauritius or of his executioners, and in any case there can be no doubt that it was long revered as a most holy relic conferring majesty on the emperor." The guidebook observed wistfully that the sword had not been used since 1916 for the crowning of the unfortunate last Habsburg emperor who parachuted into a Hungarian ditch a year later.

The medieval scabbard was a truly beautiful thing, crusted with jewels on its sheath of gold, a rare survivor from posterity's greed and debts come due. But it was only an accessory and neither the scabbard nor the sword was billed as a star attraction.

That distinction belonged to a bizarre object that reminded Regina of modern sculptures pieced together out of rusty tools and castaway junk. She had picked up its trail in her reading because of its inscription as the "Lance of the Holy Martyr St. Mauritius." Two pieces of a broken spearhead's corroded fragments about twenty inches in length were held together by an ill-fitting sheet of gold. The lettering on the sheet wrapped around the fragments—"Lance and Nail of our Lord"—covered the St. Mauritius inscription completely.

Maurizio, Mauritius, Moritz, Maurice, Regina sighed. *Whoever you are.* The sword was not inscribed with his name but only attributed to him; the spear's inscription with his name was hidden. Regina supposed that this was an ambitious medieval upgrade, a literal cover-up to transform the spear into the lance of Longinus, the legendary Roman centurion who pierced the right side of Jesus on the cross. She recalled the pious legend: the wound, instead of proving Jesus was dead, spouted water and blood foretelling salvation through baptism and the mass. Longinus was instantly converted, the first Christian convert. Reassigned from Mauritius to Longinus, the pieces of the sword were converted yet again into a reliquary for one of countless crucifixion nails.

There were other complications. The sword and the spear had multiplied in the market for relics. A rival sword in Turin originally came from the Swiss town of Saint-Maurice-en-Valais near where Mauritius had supposedly been martyred; shards revered as pieces of the true lance had turned up in Paris, Rome, and even Armenia. There was a facsimile sword in Charlemagne's capital in Aachen. All the regalia in Vienna had moved about: to Italy in imperial coronation rituals; to Prague for a hundred or so years in the 14th century; in the 15th century to the free city of Nuremberg where they were supposed to be held "in perpetuity."

The sword and spear got to Vienna relatively late. They were among the regalia sent for safekeeping from the Corsican Little Caesar who conquered more empire than the Austrian Habsburgs; the Austrian branch of the Habsburg family had won most of its empire in the marriage bed. From the records of Napoleon's handiwork she had seen in the archive Regina was sure he would have carted the regalia away as unrepentantly as he had stripped the altars and libraries in Venice.

Against all evidence to the contrary, the last sentence in the guidebook entry declared that the imperial treasures "had now come definitively to rest in their rightful home" after the "unfortunate interlude" in Nuremberg between 1938 and 1946. That was a delicate way of saying that the Nazis had packed them off to their showplace capital immediately after the German annexation of Austria in 1938. Fortunately, sword and spear hadn't worked the wonder of a third Thousand-Year Reich, but from trolling on the web Regina knew that they were still wandering restlessly in fantasy books and movies, conspiracy theories, and wishful thinking.

***

Ayse had suggested they meet late in the day to compare notes. "If the weather's good we can walk in the palace garden. Or just go for a beer in the Rathaus cellar—good in any weather."

Like the other monumental buildings on the boulevard around the city core where its old walls once stood, the Rathaus was themed to its function. It was an overblown 19th-century remake of medieval city halls, as if that would prove that the Habsburg dynasty had not been the real rulers of the city for centuries or that cheering crowds in 1938 hadn't celebrated Hitler's take over. The hefty mugs plunked down on folkish wooden tables were a cinematic detail, but as Ayse had promised, the beer didn't need staging.

"It looks like you need cheering up." Ayse saw through Regina's half-hearted smile as they toasted being in Vienna.

"I didn't get a revelation in the Treasure Room, if that's what you mean. I guess there isn't any magic left in the relics."

"Are you sure? The book I went to the library to read was full of harem poems. Circassian slave women, Sweet Perfume and White Gold; locked-up women as joyful sex slaves. Same old male fantasies, just more exotic than most. So I took a break and looked up your saint in a German citation index and found this." Ayse put a copy of a photograph on the table. It was a blurry black and white, but there was no mistaking the figure standing in profile on the right.

Adolf Hitler was wearing what looked like a khaki-colored uniform with a swastika armband. He was reaching for a sword in a scabbard covered with a lozenge shaped pattern; it was held out to him by a taller man in a darker uniform that, paunchy though he was, was too big for him. Hitler's lips were parted, evidently acknowledging the offering; the other man posed stiffly at attention with a fatuous look on his face. In the background what looked like a raised altar was covered with flowers or ribbons of some sort. Ayse translated the caption: "Unknown Photographer. Mayor Willy Liebel Presents the Sword of Empire to Hitler, Nuremberg, 1934."

"And get this, Regina. The sword in the photo is a facsimile of Moritz's sword that was in Aachen; Liebel gave Hitler a copy of that copy a year later." She paused, grinning. "The Nazis obviously didn't agree with you that it lost its magic."

Regina whistled softly. Ayse sat back to let her revelation sink in before continuing. "According to a research report on medieval art in Nazi propaganda—that's where I found the photo—Liebel had a sword cult campaign going from the early '30s on."

She slipped another photocopy onto the table. "Here's what Liebel said when he presented his copy to Hitler at the big Nazi party congress in 1935: 'Into your hands, *mein Führer*, I place the Reich Sword remade of the noblest material; receive it as our gift to the *Führer* of all Germans, who has made Germany again one Volk, strong and free, and has conferred new life on the treasure preserved for centuries in our Nuremberg as a symbol of the Unity, the Greatness, the Power, the Strength of the German Nation.'"

Regina shook her head in disbelief trying to make sense of it all. "So this mayor, this Liebel, must have been plotting all along to get the sword and the rest away from Vienna and back to Nuremberg."

"That's pretty clear. And other Nazi toadies were in on the act. The director and the chief restorer of the big National Museum in Nuremberg published pseudo-academic articles about the sword. Stuff like its being 'the symbol, the witness to history of the imperial destiny and warrior might of the German people.' Nothing about German women of course. But a lot about Nuremberg being 'the most German of all German cities, and so the rightful keeper of the sword.'"

"So they were already making this up to justify the theft in '38. You're not making any of this up, are you?"

"I told you, you really do need an anthropologist. We don't just do faraway tribes these days; the whole world's strange enough."

It was Regina's turn to amaze Ayse with her finds on the web. Links to the healing powers of the sword; advertisements for the latest replicas; the lance in church history and in fabulous myths as the "Spear of Destiny" that would rule the world. The Jews and the Masons had suppressed the Truth that Adolf Hitler started World War II to capture the spear. When the war was all but lost, true believers had conspired to substitute fakes for the real spear and the real sword; the genuine objects were sent into hiding somewhere in Europe or Latin America or maybe Antarctica. To usher in another Reich.

In an unsettling twist, Hitler's swaggering American nemesis General Patton fell under the charm of the regalia and sent a special mission to search for them in the last days of the war. They were discovered, hidden away behind a brick wall in Nuremberg. A German-born art historian, who had joined the American army and was on the mission, took credit for the discovery and embroidered on his exploits for years afterwards as a professor at Berkeley.

There was nothing about Giotto's San Maurizio in the recovered treasure trove, but from what Regina already knew about the twists and turns in the saint's history there was no telling where she might find out something else about it.

4

Regina woke late to the signal that warned of coming *acqua alta*, high water. A siren, mournful and menacing, was followed by two warning tones— meaning the lagoon would rise three feet or more at high tide. That wasn't the highest the water could get. Far from it. It had peaked, driven by the wind, much higher and stayed that way in the catastrophic 1966 flood. Since then there had been lesser incursions, but this tide would be enough to turn Piazza San Marco into a big pond. Crude plank bridges would be set up at water-logged low points. Residents would pull on rubber boots or wait until it was over; drunken study-abroad students would belly flop off bridges and try to get Italian girls to jump in with them. It was a routine inconvenience for Venetians, a sideshow for tourists, and a recurrent natural disaster.

The guidebook to the treasures Regina had seen in Vienna lay splayed out on the floor next to her bed. She had dreamed about them. Disappearing, hidden, stolen—it wasn't clear which—then turning up somewhere or other. She ran in the dream toward bright flashes, like strobe lights; she was gaining on the on-and-off shots of the Schatzkammer sword and spear that popped up in different sizes and locations. When she grasped for them, they went dark. *Basta, Regina*, she thought, rubbing her eyes when she woke up. *You were dreaming about the guy on the train too, making love to him in high water.*

Had her Vienna expedition been worth it? San Maurizio's sword and spear were overloaded with past agendas, but they looked now like curiosities displayed under glass for some forgotten purpose. So far as Regina could tell, she was the only Schatzkammer visitor who was the least bit interested. But Ayse was right. They must have been charged with an imperial aura long enough to bedazzle the Nazis. It was easier now to suppose that the saint mattered enough to Scrovegni to want his picture painted, and that Giotto would have obliged.

Ayse was a genuine treasure and the trip would have been worthwhile to know that their easy affection was intact. That wasn't exactly the way to put it. What she meant was that the independence they valued was part of the bond between them. Seeing Ayse stirred up some lingering doubts about too much independence. Regina missed her smile and her solid body; she was reminded of that all over again in Vienna. But neither of them demanded exclusive commitments. How did the Italian go? *Godere il beneficio del tempo*—yes, it was enough to enjoy the blessing of time.

Time wasn't offering her much enjoyment at the moment. The apartment felt too dark and empty and email was not satisfying company. When she logged on, she regretted it. The first message was from Terterian. It was all about his working on a script on the Borgia for PBS, a lecture on "Deconstructing the Canon in Renaissance Art," and a preview of an auction of Old Master paintings. At least he wasn't asking about her work. He probably didn't mean it that way, but she took this as a reprieve from having to tell him about the turn her research was taking. She wasn't sure herself where it was heading.

For a guilt-free distraction she lay back on the third-hand couch and switched on the TV as she sometimes did after a long day. It was a low-intensity way to improve her Italian and keep up with the erratic pulse, either racing or close to moribund, of Italian life. You could miss that in the Venetian bubble where the languages were international and the *Gazzettino* was like a small town paper.

The TV came on with Sunday night news and that meant highlights from the day's slate of soccer games. The non-stop replays always looked more or less the same to her: the bullet kick or header shot to beat a diving goalie; the victory hugs and fist-pumps and the dejected losers; the announcer drowned out by cheering fans. Just as she reached for the remote, she saw a face that actually looked familiar. It was Giovanni, from the train. He was dodging an opposing player with a quick pivot, delivering the ball kicked over to him into the net for a goal. The hip haircut, the brown skin with old acne scars, the fluid body moves as he hugged his teammates—it was him.

Regina switched her computer back on to google "Giovanni Bonelli." He played for one of Italy's storied teams, A.C. Milano. The card he had given her on the train didn't identify him beyond an email contact, but she realized he had dropped a hint as he was getting off the train at Bolzano, something about aiming for targets. Was he being charming or just playing another kind of game? Or maybe it was just her obliviousness that she hadn't picked up on it.

She reached into her little leather bag to retrieve his card. She had thought she might make contact at some point, but she didn't want to appear too available. She hadn't decided whether it would be fun to say she had discovered who he was or whether it would only be embarrassing to tell him what most people already knew.

She texted Flavia. *"Vienna was good. Will tell you about it. BTW met Giovanni Bonelli on the train."*

Flavia texted back immediately. "Better follow up right away—on Bonelli, I mean."

Regina didn't have to wait. Just then, her computer pinged. A message from Giovanni with polite expressions of pleasure at meeting her.

"I'll be in Venice next weekend for a reception; at a palazzo with quite an art collection. Would you care to go with me and perhaps have a drink before or after?"

***

Like many "new Venetians," Piergiorgio Brambilla admired the patrician style. Unlike most real patricians these days, he could afford it many times over in the Palazzo Bastagli on the Grand Canal. With his gray mane, custom-made blue blazers, and red silk ties embroidered with the lion of St. Mark, he looked the part. It would never do in Venice to be a mainland magnate from Milan. His new wife's old Venetian family name made connections easy and he could ignore the gossip.

He had become a close student of cherished Venetian exceptions that proved the rule of how things get done in Italy. If you went straight ahead in Venice, you were probably lost or going to be. One moment you were dealing with a small town, next with a world city; then with a breakaway region, a tourist Mecca, an environmental time-bomb. The finger-pointing you expect everywhere in Italy never let up in Venice. "It makes Milan look simple," he had taken to saying to Milanese friends who were incredulous that anything could be simple in their capital of Italian chic.

Money didn't matter much to him now. His people in Milan mostly took care of that. He knew they thought Venice was just his latest entertainment. *They're right*, he said to himself, looking from his balcony at the parade of preening palaces on the Grand Canal. *But they should know by now that I take my hobbies seriously*. You could buy practically anything in Milan. In Venice you had to cut a finer figure without being taken in by it. Venice was the supreme test of *la bella figura*. Brambilla aimed to master it.

He was no utopian, but he was not a pessimist either. He had not come to live in a dead city. That's what the *Venezia com'era* crowd wanted. Give them "Venice the way it was" with a dose of the old killer plagues, poverty, crumbling buildings, and peeling pictures and the tune would change.

"Save Venice" was more like it, or would be if it weren't just another carnival mask. *Maybe*, as Brambilla pictured it to himself, *as a joker with a frown that looks like a smirk upside down*. Any new emergency brought out tired accusations without making any difference. Complaints veered from manmade to natural disasters. High water, sinking land, poisoned air for the Greens; tourist masses, giant cruise ships, neighborhoods emptying out for "real Venetians"; a carping medley from foreign critics who always thought they knew better.

Some of Brambilla's Venetian friends said all the repetition was comforting. A chic woman with an old Venetian name teased him about this. "*Caro* Piergiorgio, you'll never become a real Venetian if you think things will change—for the better anyway. We are very good at proposals, but we have lots of practice at paying little attention to them. 'Save Venice' means that we can't be counted on to save ourselves."

The brittle pose was not Brambilla's style. Neither was the hypocrisy of the "true sons and daughters of San Marco" wringing their hands about "foreign invaders and new barbarians" while raking in their money under the table from illegal rents and overcharging tourists. Not really cheating of course, just doing what it takes to get by.

The "Great Projects" against flooding were like that very big time. Grandiose engineering on the lagoon required big bribes and big political payoffs. Not really cheating of course, just the cost of protecting a priceless world treasure. Good money going south from the Veneto to crooks in Calabria and Sicily, that was real crime. Venice ought to have seceded long ago, so the rant went, from the swindlers in Rome. Venice and the Veneto for the Venetians—like old times. Never mind the inconvenient truth that the republic of St. Mark got a lion's share of funding—Brambilla liked the pun—from Rome and from foreigners with fat checkbooks. Nothing new about that. Venice had always extracted or stolen what it needed. Like shit and garbage in the canals, scandals appeared, disappeared, and resurfaced periodically but smelled all the time.

It was an advantage of not being a real Venetian that he could be as independent as it suited him to be. The big operators and their spooks wanted to see him on board. Free agents were always a danger to joint stock companies of corruption. *And they know I'm not too bad at big projects.* Brambilla relished his false modesty before adding, *With the difference that mine work.* In Milan he watched football from the sidelines; in Venice he could aspire to being a manager and a player in the prestige sport of taking Venice seriously.

He raised an admonishing finger, like a coach in the locker room at halftime. *Big industries, mostly defunct now, at Porto Marghera and Mestre were going to fix things? Dams on the lagoon? Hong Kong Venice with a ring of skyscrapers around it? Disneyland instead of garbage on the island of San Biagio? Crazy and stupid too. Pazzesco!*

Brambilla had different ideas and was ready to act on them.

***

What would he be like, Regina wondered? Giovanni had proposed that they meet at a wine bar, Al Remer, and go from a drink there to the reception he had mentioned. She wasn't sure what to expect from her scattered impressions on the train, news clips, the internet, and a nice invitation. The Soccer Player and the Lady Scholar, not even a real scholar; it sounded like a bad movie. Mercifully, the tide was receding, so she could wear her only dressy pumps to go with a silvery gray dress, flattering enough for their meeting, she hoped, and elegant enough for the reception.

The place Giovanni suggested was several turns down a narrow defile from San Giovanni Crisostomo. Just when Regina was thinking she must have taken another of Cannaregio's wrong turns, she saw a niche of open space ahead. It was a miniature campo on the Grand Canal and Giovanni was waiting under a brick stairway by the door to Al Remer. He stepped forward to greet her with a "ciao" and the ritual double-cheek Italian kiss. Somewhat to her dismay she felt her heart skip a beat.

Her memory had not played tricks on her about the North African look, the dark, piercing eyes, the oddly angled smile, the fluid movement. He wasn't especially tall, big, or muscular. There was little to mark him as the athlete she now knew him to be. She had heard a soccer-loving friend of a friend holding forth on the fact—he insisted that everyone agreed—that the great players were not necessarily super-athletes, just one in a million with a gift for the game. She didn't care much whether Pele, Maradona, or Lionel Messi were so physically imposing and knew next to nothing about them anyway, but she didn't notice any conspicuous sign of Giovanni's soccer prowess besides his easiness at being at home in his body.

Her brother Brandon had taken her to some team parties when he was on a football scholarship at the University of Georgia before he blew out his knee. His teammates were nice, even sweet, for such giant strongmen. One of them had tried to get something started with her until she mentioned art history; he lost his nerve realizing he didn't have what it took to play in her league. "That's how it is," Brandon explained when she'd offered her impressions. "It's hard to get to class at all, much less study or talk with a girl like you."

She couldn't tell from their brief encounter on the train and his message, but she thought—wanted to believe anyway—that Giovanni wasn't like that.

In the flush of the moment, Regina had forgotten that he was a celebrity. No one was forward enough to come up to him. But when he led her into the wine bar with candle-lit wooden tables, she saw nudges, heads turning, phones coming out to tweet and text the sighting.

"It's on the house. Great game on Sunday." The ponytailed bartender served up two sparkling crystal glasses of ruby Amarone.

Giovanni raised his glass to Regina. "Kicking a ball around does have some benefits." She raised hers as though she had known it all along. He gestured toward the pocket-sized courtyard outside. "It'll be calmer out there." He carried their glasses with a tray of assorted cicchetti to the bench next to a little wooden dock on the canal. They were just a stone's throw from the Rialto bridge, yet tucked away almost as if—a rare sensation in Venice—they had it to themselves.

"This is better than the train." Giovanni smiled as he handed Regina's glass to her. "I had to get off too soon and you were heading to Vienna. Isn't that right?"

"Yes," Regina said after a moment's surprise. She certainly remembered but wouldn't have imagined that he did.

"Something about your going on a treasure hunt. How could I forget that?"

He really did remember then. If it was a pick-up line, it was a good one. Regina relaxed. "I probably said it was going to be a wild goose chase; you translated 'like trying to catch flies.' I did catch some after all. Not a picture of San Maurizio I'm looking for though." She wasn't sure she had mentioned San Maurizio to him before.

She was sure, however, that she shouldn't be talking shop. She was pleasantly impressed that he was in no hurry to turn the conversation to himself. She wanted to hear what it was like coming from Africa to the mountains around Pieve di Cadore and how he had got from there into bigtime soccer; something about his likes and dislikes. She wouldn't ask about the glamorous groupies around him in the tabloids.

She settled for a little flirtation. "What if I admitted that I haven't been to a real calcio game?"

Giovanni was not an amateur at this sport, either. "I'll invite you then. Whenever you like."

She wasn't interested in knowing more about soccer just then, but after she accepted the invitation, with more to look forward to, it was easy to chat. He talked about learning his game from having to stand up to the tough mountain kids; she told him a little about her version of finding her own way, growing up having to defend what people called her "unusual interests"; it went without saying, "for a person of color." It was good to feel some rapport across their differences.

"Tell me more about this party," Regina said, when he asked if she was ready to move on. "As good as this place?"

"It's in your San Maurizio's Contrada if that helps. Piergiorgio Brambilla's Palazzo Bastagli. Calcio's one of his expensive hobbies, but he's really into Venice now. He's got lots of old pictures you'll want to see."

***

Façades on the Grand Canal had always been showplaces from the outside and windows on the world from within. Piergiorgio Brambilla's favorite view, his private theater, was the bank of arched windows in his all-purpose retreat behind the Palazzo Bastagli's façade. He could see the

Baroque histrionics of the church of the Salute and the ruffled water of the Bacino in one direction; in the other, the Accademia and the makeshift wooden Accademia bridge that no one quite knew how to keep or how to replace. Brambilla was in no hurry to turn away. Hurrying was for Milan. He would let the day unfold at a Venetian pace.

Marino had brought late morning coffee to his table by the window. His wife was away with her horses in the Val Gardena. There were just a few calls to make; Venetians of a certain class had little use for email. Conversation among friends was best reserved for the late afternoon *aperitivo* with elegant snacks, the ritual *ombra* named after the shadows toward the end of the day when secrets were told over a glass. He took a second cup, unusual for him, to catch up on news in the Venice paper, *Il Gazzettino*; he had already read the *Corriere della Sera* and the *Gazzetta dello Sport*.

As usual, the *Gazzettino* was full of long-running local scandals and new ones on their way to becoming old. By the time they were reported everybody who mattered in Venice already knew about them. The rumor mill had been churning out stories about the bigtime troubles of the Consorzio Nuova Venezia for years, but nothing much had come of them except more stories. That would probably be the case again with the reports Brambilla was reading about payoffs in that consortium's contracts for the massive retractable barriers in the lagoon that were supposed to block *acqua alta*. MOSE, the nickname for those barriers, was a spin-off on Moses saving the Jews from the Red Sea; the elegant acronym for an ungainly name, *Modulo Sperimentale Elettrico Meccanico*, "Experimental Electrical Mechanical Module," acknowledged inadvertently that only a Moses miracle would make the system work. You could never be quite sure what was fiction about the project and its failings, what was true, or who knew what at any point in time. It was an unsettling fact in Italy that the news was sometimes accurate and that regulations and formalities were sometimes taken seriously.

That's why you cultivated people who could keep you ahead of the news. Brambilla's friend Paolo Michiel in the Procurator's office that investigated and prosecuted criminal cases had alerted him the week before to a break in the Consorzio case.

"So, Paolo, the choir's finally going to sing."

Michiel's hand chopped the air. "More like ready to squeal. Once one of them made a deal with us, the others practically lined up to finger the next guy. Padded bills, fake inspections. You name it. *Al culo*—fucked everybody."

"Naming everybody?"

"Not just the chumps. From the top down. Starting with His Excellency the Mayor and the bigshot *pezzi grossi* at the Consorzio. Passing around envelopes of cash even."

"Like Calabria. Should we laugh or cry that they're not shrewder up here?"

Michiel raised his palms in a gesture of appeal for justice. "Until someone gets caught. Win a few, lose a few. You know how it goes, Piergiorgio."

Yes, I do know, Brambilla said to himself as he set out late in the afternoon for an *ombra* with Gasparo Corner. That's why he was putting his Venetian project together carefully. He took the long route through Campo San Maurizio to the Gritti Palace to reassure himself about that piece of his plan.

Corner was already waiting for him at the terrace bar. Like other Venetians with old family names and dwindling resources, Corner made a career of being a useful friend. This was his only visible profession. "*Ah, Piergiorgio. Come stai, caro mio?*" He glanced at Brambilla's carefully groomed but slightly windswept Venetian look set off by the ivory shirt and a bespoke navy jacket tailored at the elegant La Barena men's boutique. "Very well, I see. Venice obviously agrees with you. I believe you'll want that favorite single malt of yours?"

"And you'll have your Spritz, Gasparo."

"Just another tourist drink now, I'm afraid. Nothing's sacred anymore."

Corner already knew the answer to his next question. "You saw this morning's *Gazzettino* on the Consorzio business?"

"With three reporters saying the same thing I couldn't miss it. It's about time they got around to what they already knew."

"This won't create problems for you will it, Piergiorgio." Corner paused for his appreciation to be noticed. "No, of course not."

Brambilla ignored the fawning. "Just distractions for them. The prosecutors indict a few *pezzi grossi* and sacrifice some middlemen, and everybody else will run for cover until it's safe to start up the old racket again."

"Yes, the same old racket."

"They spend 6 billion euros, and still counting, fifty years too late to put dams under water in the lagoon that are probably not going to work. Or cause more damage if they do."

Corner had the next lines down pat. "What happens when the lagoon backs up? Or the monster cruise ships drag bottom? Envelopes of cash. So crude." He put on a comic imitation of a straight face. "But come now, Piergiorgio. What about those glossy posters around town? Beautiful new beaches, new resorts on the islands, culture, ecology for all." Corner concluded with the flourish he knew Brambilla would like to hear. "Seriously now, Piergiorgio, all those follies out on the lagoon—they make your projects look that much better."

***

Regina and Giovanni walked under the triumphal arch of a portal into the courtyard of the Palazzo Bastagli. The uniformed doorman directed them to the monumental stairway that turned at the landing in the opposite direction toward the long hall on the *piano nobile,* the show floor running the length of the building. Chandeliers of coiled Murano glass, a polychrome marble pavement, and rows of darkening pictures paraded toward the cluster of high windows opening onto the Grand Canal.

This was a far cry from Regina's Venice of graying plaster, loose bricks, and warped shutters that that wouldn't quite close. It was patrician Venice, except that there weren't many real patricians left. The old palazzo sparkled and gleamed a little too brightly, like a photo spread in a high-end magazine.

The guests were to match. Brambilla's invitations to the Palazzo Bastagli were much sought after. He made sure of that. As Giovanni had promised, the occasion was not full-dress formal, so no tuxes and evening dresses. Italy heavy on gold and diamonds, plastic surgery, and HGH was somewhere else tonight. This was mostly a select, polished crowd. The sartorial standards ran to open-collared silk shirts and suits for the men with plenty of elegant Cady Selena, Versace, and Bottega Veneta concoctions among the women. The single gays and gay couples were conspicuously but comfortably elegant. Regina was pleased to notice that glances in her direction were more interested than dismissive.

Giovanni had told her something about Brambilla and how he liked to tweak the Venetian caste system. This was a scandal to people with old family names and people with new money, particularly when they were not invited to the Palazzo Bastagli. A cosmopolitan mix, always hard-edged in Milan, was more civil and easier to produce in Venice, give or take some predictable backbiting. Brambilla played the patrician patron with restraint. He did not intend to be, he had told Giovanni in an unguarded moment, the Cavalier of Clowns that Silvio Berlusconi had become.

It being Italy, though, he had to be careful about politics. Regina already knew from her occasional reading in the *Gazzettino* that a real Venetian could not be a modern day Machiavelli. The veneer of Venetian civic responsibility was a constraint and the ruthless efficiency of the old regime had long since given way to political amateurism. It did not take much reading of local news to see that Venetians of every political stripe believed they were fully entitled to rule themselves while regularly making a mess of trying to do so.

Self-serving myths were a Venetian tradition. Regina didn't need to remind herself that myth-making was American too. She didn't think of herself as political, unless that meant being wary about politics. She knew this was a luxury that the civil rights generations of her parents and grandparents made possible. She had no illusions that it was bound to last. "Land of the Free" was just one American mantra overburdened with too much to compensate for. She would have to make the best of it while she could.

The old myths of Venice were still sprouting fertile variations. True believers claimed that they were the descendants of a chosen race of "Padanians"; that the Italian nation state unified in 1870 was a swindle; that the gravelly voices of the separatist politicians of the Northern League were gospel; that Rome siphoned off all the profits of the Veneto to its corrupt clients in the south of Italy. A few hard core types went in for antics like reclaiming Piazza San Marco with a cannon mounted on a tractor, but it was enough for most Venetian politicians to hang the banner of San Marco from a balcony and endorse negotiations, separatist referendums, or some "federal solution" to autonomy for Venice and the Veneto.

Glasses of prosecco had been raised to such proposals before at the Palazzo Bastagli. Not long after Regina and Giovanni arrived, Brambilla tapped on his glass to call for the attention of his guests. "It is a pleasure to welcome so many good friends. Especially on this occasion. I have asked you here tonight to share some thoughts about this incomparable city."

A few "good friends" looked away more or less discreetly at the thought of sharing their city with this immigrant from Milan.

"Large visions are second nature to Venice next to nature itself—the great lagoon. But we know ourselves by neighborhoods, as, for example, here, in the Contrada of San Maurizio. I do not wish in any way to diminish large ambitions, as you will know"—there was a pause here; no one could imagine small ambitions of him—"but only to say that the smaller ones are inseparable from the energy, the enterprise of the whole. This is easily forgotten and, dare I say, has been forgotten with painful results—grand projects with fewer results and exorbitant expenses with what it might be too delicate to call the liabilities that those great projects have repeatedly brought upon the city." Everyone understood the allusions: the indictment of the Consorizio operation and their own feeble consciences about selling out the city to the highest bidders.

Brambilla went on to outline what he called a "San Maurizio Initiative," inspired, he said, by what the old Venetians had done. The Campo just up Rio San Maurizio from the Palazzo Bastagli had seen better days, but it had the intimate proportions, the church, and the ancient wellhead of a neighborhood that cried out to be brought back to life again. It was off the main tourist track but not far from Piazza San Marco and the Grand Canal.

With some care, it would be a discovery for travelers who liked to think they had found a place only the locals knew about. The Campo was already the site of an antiquarian fair at different times of year; the church housed an impressive collection of stringed instruments. The Palazzo Zaguri could be restored. As a cultural center hard to find in Venice. Not the extravaganza, not the palace converted into a corporate showplace no one needed, not yet another museum or luxurious hotel.

The empty buildings around the Campo could be renovated as affordable housing near the center of the city for artisans and young professionals, to get a market going—better that than new blights of public housing or another Mestre. It would be a civil, cosmopolitan place where Venetians, new and old, and their visitors would mingle and mix. It would not be the fake Venice of mask shops and the luxury trade or the fussy sanctuary of Save Venice and haughty foreigners or one more bad design by the Faculty of Architecture. Yes, the Campo was admittedly vulnerable to *acqua alta,* but committing to it now would be a vote of confidence in future controls.

There was some uncomfortable rustling in crowd at this point, but Brambilla pressed on. "There will be something good and true in this new initiative for everybody."

He concluded with a teaser. "And with its success, we can turn with proven confidence to renovations of the stadium at Sant'Elena and plans for a state-of-the-art sports complex on the north side of the lagoon."

It was not a demonstrative crowd. Some buzz of disbelief and disapproval was covered by polite applause and the clink of toasting glasses.

After a decent interval, people resumed their conversations or moved on. Giovanni asked Regina if she would like to meet their host, who had joined a small circle of listeners or admirers. The difference wasn't clear. Brambilla was obviously used to commanding the attention that came from being, according to the latest magazine rankings, one of Italy's richest men.

"Ah, Giovanni. A pleasure to see you," he said, inviting him into the circle with easy authority. The informal *tu* didn't sound condescending. It was clear that they were on good terms. "And who is your lovely companion?"

Giovanni introduced Regina around as an American historian of art doing important research in Venice, "who knows all about Renaissance pictures." The group smiled politely, either at the exaggeration or doubting that an art historian, least of all a black American woman, could be doing much of importance. Lots of up-to-date Italians would rather vacation with Club Med or in the Greek islands than look at old pictures. Regina had met Romans who had never been in the Sistine Chapel and Venetians who hadn't visited the Accademia since a school field trip.

58

She didn't let herself be flustered. "I don't know about the importance and there's always more to learn in Venice." She turned toward her host. "This evening, for example, in your toast about Campo San Maurizio. I'm interested right now in Maurizio myself. A Bellini drawing of him in Paris. Maybe a painting of him in Venice, much earlier, close to Giotto."

Brambilla looked at Regina appraisingly. "Unfortunately, dottoressa, I don't have any Bellinis." He actually knew something about art? "And Giotto's circle in Venice... I've never heard it said that he got closer than Padua. Maybe you know better. I'm sure this guy," Brambilla winked at Giovanni, "can spare you for a few hours. Why don't we talk about this another time?"

Regina glanced over at her companion, not that she needed encouragement. When Giovanni turned to another guest, Brambilla assured her that it would be a pleasure to see her again. Perhaps next week after he returned from visiting his wife in the Val Gardena. Regina checked the urge to say that she could hardly wait. "It's kind of you to take an interest in my work," she said, reaching into her bag for one of the calling cards the Bangladeshi copy shop had printed for her.

The novelty of mingling with the posh crowd lost whatever charm it had after that. She and Giovanni circulated awhile longer. One couple regaled them with stories about the poor valet parking on a recent ski trip to Davos and their son's accomplishments at Harvard; his MBA, Wall Street connections, American girl friends. Perhaps too many girlfriends. The Italian mother worried that none of them would be suitable for him and—this is what she really meant without saying it—acceptable to her. To Regina's great relief Giovanni signaled he was ready to liberate her from another round of braggadocio.

***

"Thanks," Regina mouthed as Giovanni guided her toward the intarsia-paneled door beneath the coat-of-arms of a patrician family that had cashed out long ago. One of Brambillla's staff opened it discreetly. Regina couldn't have dreamed up such a fantasy date, much less the invitation to return to the Palazzo Bastagli. She basked in the glow of anticipation, the Amarone, and a few glasses of prosecco.

Giovanni took her arm as they started down the grand staircase. "It's still early. How about a nightcap?" She had thought of it herself, but Venetian nightlife was limited, her experience of it more so. She had already had enough of a crowd scene. Her apartment wouldn't do, the upstairs studio perfumed by mildew in the dim flickering light of neon bulbs; even Casanova would have balked at a liaison there. In any case she wasn't sure how far she wanted to act out her fantasies, even in Venice where fleeting romances and casual sex were nothing to wonder about unless they didn't happen.

She tried to balance her openness and independence—they were not the same in her mind—in these matters as in most things. She had boyfriends and a sex life of her choosing, including that semester with Ayse. Race wasn't a big issue, at least for her. Her first serious love-making came during a hot Atlanta summer with Brad, a white high school classmate. At Spelman she dated black guys on social occasions sponsored by the college to foster a black leadership class. Her best male friends in graduate art history were gay. She was not looking for a long term partner, but she was not averse to the possibility either.

Giovanni rescued her again, this time from thinking too much about making decisions. As they descended the stairs, he told her that he was borrowing a friend's apartment; it was nearby. "You'll be interested in the view," he added with that intriguing smile.

From the Palazzo Bastagli he led her onto the Fondamenta Correr along the Rio di San Maurizio toward the Calle Zaguri. It was familiar territory for Regina. They walked a short distance along the narrow walkway to a palazzo in the Campo San Maurizio that looked out onto the saint's church. Marcella's yoga studio was upstairs just two doors away.

A freshly painted green door and polished brass signaled a world of difference from the entrance to Marcella's studio. Giovanni turned the key and stepped aside. The spacious foyer was a marvel with its polished marble paving, a domed ceiling, and well-proportioned niches around the walls. There was an old-fashioned elevator across the way that, judging from the perfect condition of the elevator cage, looked like it actually worked.

"It's on the top floor," Giovanni said, pulling aside the shiny brass scissor doors. "Be my guest."

The apartment in a high loft had been remodeled for a contemporary look with a Venetian accent. There were terrazzo floors, a Bokhara carpet, a soft beige leather sofa and matching armchairs. The walls were painted in pastels with ivory trim. A tray of liqueurs and glasses sat on a glass coffee table. The view through the windows worked wonders; even the façade of the church looked good.

"I can't believe this!" The privileged height and the night lighting improved the view Regina was familiar with beyond recognition. The peeling doors, the outlet shop with a tacky yellow banner, the empty palazzo across the way could hardly be made out, imagined even. Another San Maurizio miracle. Brimming with pleasure, she turned back from the view. Giovanni had poured two small crystal glasses of grappa. They toasted the saint.

There was no mistaking their signals after that. With no preamble he leaned in to kiss her on the mouth. She drew him close, running her hand across the lean muscle of his back. He deepened the kiss, exploring her body, until, pulling away, he reached to unfasten her dress. She let the dress and her slip fall around her ankles, kicked off her pumps and reached down for him as he guided her hand. They sank down on the cushions from sofa and melted into one another in long drawn out love-making.

Regina woke first, only half-remembering being carried to the bed. It was a dull grey outside, no streaming Tiepolo light announcing the day. The grinding vaporettos down on the Grand Canal were an unforgiving alarm clock. She spooned up to Giovanni, lacing her arms around his chest. She was not going to launch into morning-after doubts. What did he want from her? A one-night stand? What did she want? Could they make something together across their differences? Regina had no idea.

It didn't matter for now. She was too caught up for compatibility tests. She dismissed one that came up after he pulled her over for morning love-making—that he would have to get to Milan for the afternoon walk-through.

***

Before his Palazzo Bastagli reception Piergiorgio Brambilla had not said much of anything in public about his plans for Campo San Maurizio. He had not said everything then. The Campo was the center of his chosen neighborhood now, but there was a more intimate connection.

Families like his had stories about family art treasures mysteriously disappearing, lost to crooked dealers, sold on the cheap for gambling debts, coveted by greedy relatives. Brambilla's Uncle Maurizio had once hinted that the story didn't have to turn out like that. His nephew would see soon enough.

"Does the family know about this?" Brambilla had asked, supposing that he must have been left out of the loop for some reason.

"Better they don't. You don't want your cousins to make off with whatever else they can. Just like their mother. Anyway, I'm not talking about family property. It's about something that came to me at the end of the war. You've heard the stories, but you don't really know what it was like back then. The bombings from one side then the other, killings by one side then the other, not knowing whether to trust anyone or where your next meal was coming from, if it came; people hiding things if they had anything to hide and other people rummaging to find them."

Maurizio didn't mention the Resistance and partisans. The family had gone from being prudent Fascists to being prudent neutrals when the Germans took over in '43; then converted into prudent patriots when the

Allies were winning. He went on. "You had to be a fanatic or a fool not to see what was coming. The Fascists burned their black shirts; the Germans said they were just obeying orders. The smart ones swore that if they hadn't bravely disobeyed, things would have gone worse than they did. The smartest ones made deals with the things they had saved—stolen mostly—and disappeared."

Brambilla was not sure where this was leading. "So you found something? Or bought something?" This was a delicate way of putting it. "Drawings. Paintings. A piece of sculpture maybe?"

"Not exactly. Let's say I was given a reward for helping a friend of a friend who had to leave the country in a hurry and couldn't take it with him. My friend liked to say that the gift might make a believer even out of a hardened old sinner like me. You will know more in due course."

That's all Uncle Maurizio would say. The conversation resumed with further swipes at ungrateful relatives, the rapacious ones and those who voted for the Left, which amounted to the same thing. Brambilla had all but forgotten about the occasion until it came back to him reading the letter his uncle left with his lawyer for his nephew to open after his death.

> *My dear nephew. You will remember our conversation about family art treasures. I do not intend to mention in my will what we talked about, as you can well understand. However, you should know more now as the heir of a certain work of art—you were right about that of course. One such object was the panel that you will find in a vault in Geneva; the address and access codes are written on the back of this sheet. You may have the pleasure of the picture that I thought it best to forego because of the difficult circumstances, shall we say, of how it was obtained and the insatiable cupidity of your cousins.*

In light of "difficult circumstances" Brambilla had kept whatever pleasure he took from the picture for himself. But his uncle was long since dead; the law would likely come down on his side against his cousins, if they were so foolish as to challenge him. It was time to take credit for the picture's recovery. He would promise to return it to the saint's church as proof of his attachment to Venice and his neighborhood. It would be his special pleasure to show the Consorzio gang how the old-style patrician *bella figura* was done.

***

Giovanni texted Regina with apologies for leaving her so abruptly for Milan. She let herself be reassured that she was not a castaway already. She needed a pause anyway. To try to sort through what she expected of him and of herself. And there was Piergiorgio Brambilla's invitation to talk about San Maurizio, whatever he had meant by that.

He had sent her a note—not an email but handwritten—asking her to join him for what he described as an informal *ombra*. "Not an interview or an inquisition," he had written, whether to put her at her ease or on her mettle. Probably some of both. Regina didn't know which, but she would find out soon enough.

One of his staff—not in uniform this time—met her at the portal of the Palazzo Bastagli and escorted her up the staircase to the long hall's entrance. Her host met her with that seemingly natural but studied Italian charm. Leading her in a leisurely fashion down the hall, he gestured here and there to the line-up of mythological and biblical scenes of indeterminate age and condition. Regina recognized remakes of Titian and Tintoretto mixed in with what might be 18th-century originals challenging one another in grandiosity.

At the end of the long hall Brambilla ushered her into a modestly sized room on the Grand Canal side of the palazzo. Things he obviously cared about were there. The armchairs and sofa looked comfortable. The walnut trestle table—it looked like he used it as a desk—was simple and gilt-free; the hangings on the wall left pictorial bombast to the hall of state. A round table with a simple linen cloth was set between the armchairs and sofa for the late afternoon ritual of prosecco and cicchetti.

Brambilla was in no hurry. They exchanged small talk as he poured flutes of wine which, he noted in passing, came from his private reserve in Valdobbiadene. How was she settling into Venice? The weather was always a conversation piece in Venice as were favorite places away from the crowds. Were there private collections he might help her see? When he finally brought up San Maurizio it was as if had just then remembered why they were meeting. "I was delighted, dottoressa, to learn that you have taken an interest in our saint and his little parish. There are so many others. The old Venetians made sure of that."

Regina picked up on the cue. "But Maurizio really is remarkable. Even as saints go. Commander of a Roman legion; Egyptian martyr with his soldiers for not fighting Christian rebels in the Alps; patron saint of the Holy Roman Empire." She glanced expectantly across at him. "But you know all that already."

"A little, not all. You have, so to say, a professional interest and I'm only a curious amateur. Won't you have another cicchetto? I recommend the artichoke heart; it's from Sant'Erasmo and especially good just now. Or the *granceola*, spider crab, from our lagoon."

Regina studied the delicacies to give herself time to consider her answer. "Not really professional enough, I'm afraid. Coming to have a professional interest, you might say. And still learning."

She paused, then reached to take a manila folder from her bag. "I came here loving the Bellini painters; trying to understand what people in their time wanted in the wonderful things they made." Opening the folder, she handed Brambilla a copy of the drawing she had mentioned at the reception. "But Maurizio keeps turning up. This drawing looks like Giovanni Bellini's work and it's inscribed, there at the bottom, "Mauritius.""

Brambilla held the photocopy at arm's length, drew it in for closer inspection, then handed it back. "You're convinced then? Bellini and Maurizio together, both of them?"

"I admit he doesn't look like much of a warrior. But that could be the elegant Bellini touch. His skin is white in the drawing and Maurizio's is mostly black in art, not always though." She paused deliberately. "It seems that people were anxious about his color." Seeing that Brambilla had not missed the point, she went on. "Maybe that's why someone inscribed his name. It might be a wishful attribution, a guess, maybe a forgery. That happens."

"I see you don't jump to conclusions. Admirable, dottoressa. I'm told it would not be surprising if some signatures on our pictures and some attributions to this or that artist are, shall we say, optimistic. Would you agree?"

Regina was not about to risk an opinion. She cut back to the drawing. "All in all, the style, the details, the inscription fit together well enough."

"And the things he's holding?"

"The palm branch, a martyr's symbol. The sword and spear—Maurizio's usually shown with one or the other or both together. The emperors took them over as symbols of their divine right to rule from the 12th century on."

Regina hesitated. "It sounds unbelievable, I know." She knew she should stop but it was too late. "I mean that the Nazis adopted Maurizio. They transferred—they didn't say 'stole'—his relics with other treasures of the old empire from Vienna and showed them off in Nuremberg. To prove they had inherited the imperial mission."

Brambilla, who had listened attentively, looked away, tapped the arm of his chair with his fingers slowly, first one arm, then the other. Apparently satisfied, he rose, moving toward the windows overlooking the Grand Canal and saying something quietly that Regina could not quite make out. Something like "even more remarkable than I supposed." He turned back. "I believe you can tell me more."

She was caught off balance. It wasn't clear whether he was asking or demanding. Either way, she couldn't very well dodge after telling him so much already. And in the flush of longing to share her excitement she was past resisting.

"There is," she began slowly, "some new evidence. About an early painting of Maurizio given to the saint's church. Probably a bid for the saint's blessings on your neighborhood and the donor of course." Brambilla waited with easy equanimity.

"The donor was the same man who commissioned Giotto. In Padua, the Arena Chapel. Enrico Scrovegni. He lived somewhere near you, maybe even in Campo San Maurizio." Regina stopped short of her discovery in the archive. "I don't have all the pieces together yet. I'm following up as many leads as I can."

"I see," Brambilla said, reflecting for a long moment, evidently considering how to act on what she had said.

Finally, stepping toward the wall opposite the windows, he reached under the molding on the ivory white wainscoting. "I believe you will be interested in this." A panel opened onto a shallow compartment. He lifted the silk cover to reveal the painting of a white knight in armor with sword and spear and his companions on a shimmering gold background.

***

Brambilla's launch was waiting when Regina came through the Palazzo Bastagli's courtyard. She thanked the driver, telling him that she would enjoy the walk back through Cannaregio. The truth was that she felt like she could walk on water. She wanted someone to know right away about what she had just seen. Flavia maybe, but the chances of keeping the news confidential that way would be better if Regina shouted it out to startled passersby on the Strada Nova.

Of course she would have to talk to Terterian. It was time, past time really. She could tell him about seeing the picture; fill him in later with as much background as seemed necessary. But she didn't have more excuses for delaying now. It would still be afternoon on the East Coast in the U.S. She texted to see if he was available to talk. She knew she shouldn't have added but did anyway: *BTW I may have just seen a lost Giotto.*

The ping of his message came as she was leaving Vino Vero, her favorite Cannaregio wine bar, with a celebratory bottle: "You what?! Call me." Heading for her apartment, she texted back. "OK. In a few minutes."

Terterian picked up on the first ring. "Regina, what's going on? Are you alright?"

"I'm not sure. I just saw a painting that might be a Giotto, or something close. Of San Maurizio."

"I see. You're delusional. Dissertation Stress Disorder."

Where to start when things had gone so far so fast? "Well, there was a reception at the Palazzo Bastagli, just off the Sant'Angelo vaporetto stop. It belongs to this rich, sixty-something rich Milanese who wants to be a

Venetian. He talked about the neighborhood around Campo San Maurizio, how he wants to revive it. So when someone introduced me, I said I was interested in San Maurizio myself. There's that drawing of him in the link to the Bellini article you sent me. Something offhand like that. He took me seriously. So he invited me to come back and he showed me the picture."

"Showed you the picture. Just like that. No foreplay…"

She did not appreciate the innuendo. She had just proved she could take care of herself by not mentioning anything about meeting in Brambilla's private quarters or about Giovanni. And by leaving Terterian speechless for once. "He did mention," she said archly, "that he didn't have any Bellinis."

"But he did just happen to have a Giotto. Let me get this straight. You tell him that you're interested in San Maurizio. So he shows a picture to you and you do the connoisseur. Looks like San Maurizio alright. And like Giotto too."

"Hard to believe, I know, but it really was something like that. There's a saint in armor in the center of some soldiers with a sword and spear in the picture. They're full length, maybe from a middle panel of an altarpiece, not a big one for a high altar—it's about 30 by 24 inches—maybe for private prayers or a side chapel."

Terterian stopped her. "About Giotto. Did Brambilla actually say that someone had attributed it to him? Why did you think Giotto? There are even more fights about Giotto panels than about the frescoes."

"But there really is a Giotto look in—how to put it—the *gravity* of those figures. And then"—she had to say it—"there's a document suggesting that Enrico Scrovegni commissioned a picture of San Maurizio." She left it at that. "And wouldn't it be like Giotto to have brought wispy groups of warrior saints in Crusader art from the East to the West? And even with the gold background, planted them on solid footing and made sober Romans out of them? They're all white."

5

"Do call me, John." John Terterian was not surprised to hear Phyllis Farber's plummy accent on his voicemail. "About this supposed Giotto turning up in Venice. You're the first person I thought to ask about it." That was pure Phyllis. Terterian was just one "first person" in her network.

It was her business to stay on top of the high-end New York art market. The buzz had shifted as the one percent found more up-to-date hobbies. Old masterworks that were not already languishing in museums had disappeared into the villas of oil sheiks and the stashes of offshore oligarchs in Geneva, London, or high-rise New York. But that meant that pieces otherwise unknown or passed over could come out of the woodwork, sometimes quite literally. It also meant that the competition was fierce. There was a new race of thirty-something "advisers" and "consultants," some of them even younger, who didn't stick to any one turf; many but not all of them thought Picasso was an "old master" and wouldn't know what a well-thumbed rolodex looked like. Farber maneuvered adroitly between the old club of professional dealers, her office at Satterby's, and the aggressive new breed. She was in her element at the moment, tracking rumors of the discovery of an early Renaissance masterpiece and holding another in reserve.

The news from Venice had gone from rumor into print just the day before. It was classic Italian journalism, with a shell of dark conspiracy and purple prose covering an absence of hard facts. The local Venetian paper, *Il Gazzettino*, wanted readers to believe that it was privy to a leak trickling out from an unnamed source. The reporter could trust their engrained habit of supposing that a behind-the-scenes exposé guaranteed the truth of the story. He had been told, off the record, "that a stupendous discovery would soon be announced that was certain to intrigue and delight lovers of art in Venice and throughout world." A painting "very likely from the hand of Giotto" had come to light, the first and only work painted for Venice by the great master. The details would be forthcoming soon, but expectations ran high that "we shall be able to celebrate the homecoming of a glorious masterpiece of a heroic martyr-saint to his very own church in *La Serenissima*."

Farber knew how easily speculations turned into certainties. She had bet on that move herself. It was too soon to tell how it would turn out this time. When Terterian returned her call, she went straight to the point. "Ah,

John. Now do tell me about this Venetian picture. Of San Maurizio, they say. Supposedly by Giotto no less. I'm sure you know all about it."

Terterian had sparred with Phyllis before, sometimes to keep her guessing, sometimes withholding whatever worked to his advantage. "This is out of my field, Phyllis. Out of my league even. You want a Giotto scholar. That might be a problem, though. They don't agree on much."

"Come now, John." Terterian knew she wouldn't be put off so easily. He changed tack.

"Actually there is something else."

"Didn't I know I could count on you, John? Something else you say. Enough for us to believe this Venice picture is the real thing? By Giotto? I don't need a Giotto scholar to tell me that's not going to work."

"What about an actual picture? I've heard from someone in Venice who has seen it."

"Some picture, you mean." Farber's dismissiveness couldn't conceal her curiosity. "Someone in Venice, you say."

"Yes, Regina Payne."

"Your graduate student. And she knows it's Giotto there and then. Maybe I do need a Giotto expert. "

"There's more to it from what she says."

"So tell me."

"She was invited to a party on the Grand Canal. In a palazzo of some rich Milanese collector of people and things who has settled in Venice."

"Piergiorgio Brambilla. Is that right?" Farber broke in, knowing perfectly well that it was.

Terterian let this pass. Her network was the best in the business. "He gave a little speech about his plans for his neighborhood in Venice, Campo San Maurizio. It's just off the Grand Canal, close to Piazza San Marco. Regina got herself introduced and told him that there was some new evidence that might link Giotto to San Maurizio. He invited her to come for a chat about it and it ended with him showing her the picture."

"Pardon me, John. All you know comes from your Regina finding a scrap of evidence and flirting with the great man."

"Does that make it unbelievable?"

Farber sat back for effect before trumping the question. "Would you believe me if I said there may be two Giotto San Maurizios? You had better get your Regina over here right away."

***

Terterian met Regina in front of Satterby's New York glass palace. The glass storeys were iconic of the art world, alternately glittery and opaque. Phyllis Farber had invited them—summoned was more like it—to meet at ten. It was a few minutes after the hour when they headed to the bank of elevators in the atrium.

Regina had taken the Delta red-eye from Venice. She was too keyed up to care much about sleeping. She rationalized that she would gain six hours on the time difference to New York. And even with off-and-on internet connections, she would have time for more googling on Phyllis Farber. She had checked out her profile already: stylish, fifty-something; academic and museum credentials before moving to the market side; high-end dealmaker for Old Master paintings, freelancing or working for the auction houses. There were some links to articles of hers on second-tier Renaissance art and some reports about deals she had managed for Satterby's. Her sales record had reportedly fallen off; according to the grapevine, she was past her prime. But the junior art sharks who were raiding the market would say something like that. Anyway, Regina was not going to be beaten on appearances. She had packed an elegantly understated dress to change into at JFK as protection against the Farber flair she expected.

"Phyllis isn't used to waiting," Terterian said. "She's got a Devil in Prada streak. But don't worry. She'd wait all day to find out what you've got to tell her."

Regina was relieved that Terterian seemed easy with her. She knew it was a measure of how serious the Giotto business had become that he had arranged the meeting and seen to it that her expenses were paid in advance. He was on leave and oversubscribed as usual, finishing a book, filming a PBS documentary, and, she was sure, keeping up a busy nightlife. He would have had plenty of excuses to back off.

Farber met them on the 20th floor. "Ah, here you are then," she sang out as she approached in a slimming gray silk dress that was, Regina guessed, indeed a Prada. Her perfectly colored hair and careful makeup were meant to defy the rumors on the grapevine. "Always lovely to see you, John. And Regina, I appreciate your coming on short notice." She led them to the corner office where the perfect Mies chairs framed a perfect view of the upper Eastside. "It's such a culture shock too, New York after Venice; or the other way around when we go for the Biennale. How long have you been in that floating wonder?"

Regina didn't agree about New York and Venice. Both loomed improbably out of the water, part genuine spectacle and part hype. "I'm really still learning my way around."

"Oh?" Farber said. The arch of her threaded eyebrows gave her a permanently disdainful look. "That's not what John tells me. We want to learn from you. He has explained why I wanted to meet you of course."

"That you are interested in hearing first hand about the San Maurizio picture."

"Very interested, yes. You may be the only outsider who has actually seen it."

"I don't know. Maybe others have."

"They are likely to soon."

"I suppose so, but Piergiorgio Brambilla—the painting is his—didn't say anything about what he meant to do with it. Just showed it to me."

"Yes?"

"I didn't have all that much time with it. He didn't give me a chance to take photographs, but he let me look at it closely. What I saw was pretty convincing. Old wood; vertical segments pieced together; wooden supports attached on the back; about 30 by 24 inches. A gabled frame, gilded, with a trefoil molding insert. The central figures are a haloed soldier in gilded armor with four companions turning toward him in different poses. Tempera with the right-looking pigments from what you could see through the patina and varnish; punched gold background."

Farber nodded approvingly. "I see you're not one of the new breed that gets stuck in some dingy archive. Forgetting to look and not knowing what they're seeing when they do."

"Actually I have done some archival research." Regina had decided that she could mention the document without going into specifics. She wanted to be credible with Terterian and Farber and didn't want to stretch her conscience too thin. Besides, it would be a reality check to see if they thought she was on the right track. The exact location of the document wouldn't matter to them, for the time being anyway, and no one would be rummaging around for it in such an unlikely source as the records of Napoleon's dirty work.

"Go on."

"It seems that Enrico Scrovegni gave a painting of San Maurizio to the saint's Venetian church. Scrovegni was the patron who commissioned the Arena Chapel in Padua from Giotto and…"

Farber cut her off. "Yes, of course he was. But that doesn't prove anything about Giotto. Or that the picture you saw is the one in the document."

Terterian eased in diplomatically. "Let me try a little art history here. Regina says there are some standing figures around a central one. You don't find that on panels so early, not already in Giotto's time, not in the West anyway."

"But then," Terterian spread his arms wide, "the merciful art historian—there are some, you know—might come to the rescue. He riffs on the idea that the painting takes cues from pictures brought from the Holy Land by the Crusaders and Venetian merchants. Icons and scenes in manuscripts with an armored saint or Jesus himself in the middle of a group. So a remake of the Greek look could be evidence of Giotto's

70

brilliance. With a consummate stroke of invention he enlarged such a group and moved it up to a main panel instead of putting it, as you would expect, in a little predella scene on the bottom of an altarpiece. You know how the Italians would put it: *Se non è vero, è ben trovato.*"

Farber, calmer now, glossed the Italian: "It may not be true, but it ought to be." Close enough, I believe. Thank you, John, for letting Giotto be the genius we want to believe in."

She turned to Regina. "But San Maurizio? Why do you think it's him?"

"The right props mostly: knight's armor, sword, spear, martyr's palm branch."

Farber raised a threaded eyebrow. "Mostly?"

"There's old varnish." Regina hesitated. "But the figures look white." She paused again. "But maybe that's not a problem. Maurizio looks white in some pictures, black in others."

"Interesting," Farber rose. "Please follow me." She opened the door to a hallway that looked like a museum corridor with price tags on the exhibits instead of captions. The auction rooms were discreetly located off the corridor that ran above the cashiers' windows which were out of sight on the floors below. Farber led the way to one of Satterby's intimate viewing rooms staged as private parlors with no hint of the marketplace. Crystal glasses were arranged with canapés on a silver tray on a low table. The Louis XVI décor was an interior decorator's all-purpose setting for showing off old masterpieces.

After pouring glasses of white wine, Farber walked slowly over to the easel in the corner and pulled back a velvet cover. "So what do we make of this?" She stood back, turning to observe the effect.

Regina caught her breath. She was looking at a painting much like the one she had seen in Venice. Except that the dark features of the central figure and his men stood out against the shine of their helmets. This San Maurizio—it had to be him—was black.

Farber broke the spell after a calculated interval. "Rather special, don't you agree? I'm afraid I can't tell you much about it yet. Let's say for now that it speaks for itself." It was clear that she meant to be speaking for it in the future and that, as far as she was concerned, the conversation was over. She replaced the cover carefully and ushered Terterian and Regina out toward the atrium with a few anticlimactic pleasantries about keeping in touch as "this fascinating case develops."

They couldn't talk on the elevator with other passengers getting on and off. When they got to the sidewalk, Terterian burst out, "Wasn't that something! You expect a good show from Phyllis, but she outdid herself this time." Regina, still recovering, didn't have an answer when he added, joking or all too serious, "So what do you make of being in the middle of a huge art world mystery?"

"I don't know yet," Regina answered after some indecision because she really didn't know. "But I don't think much depends on me at this point. Farber is making it her business now."

"Meaning now that you've delivered your goods, not to put too fine a turn on it. There's a lot nobody knows yet. Phyllis has already asked me for some talking points and a short list of experts."

Regina turned to look him in the eye.

"Don't worry. You can trust me."

Regina was glad she hadn't shared the location of her archival find with anybody. It might keep her in the game.

***

Jeremy Hammond was another "first person to call" on Phyllis Farber's list. He was a new assistant curator for early European painting at the Met. After the celebrity director's long reign, there was a tug-of-war in that Vatican of the American museum world. Hammond was a good compromise, neither American nor Continental; British, youngish, up-to-date but not insistently so. His tailored Jermyn Street look made up for his perpetual three-day-old stubble and he was comfortable enough with the old rituals. He seemed the perfect choice for Farber to test the waters at the Met.

Off-the-record lunches were all in a day's work for museum staff and the art trade. The Hotel Carlyle bar with its Bemelmans murals of high jinks in Central Park was a trading zone for gossip and strategic leaks. Farber was a regular there. She was already settled with a Dom Perignon on ice when Hammond was ushered across the invisible cord of privilege to her table.

Hammond described the scene the next day for the amusement of his two closest colleagues at the Met. He trusted them to keep a confidence in the rumor mill of staff offices, at least for a decent interval. They had survived the mysterious hiring rites a few years earlier but were not yet old hands with free ranging gossiping privileges. Dara Levy worked in the conservation lab; Malcolm Sargeant was an associate curator of medieval painting. They had made a point of teaching him the ropes without his having to ask, and he needed their advice now.

"OK, Jeremy," said Dara in an unrepentant Brooklyn accent as he cleared away the remnants of a brown bag lunch. "A humble working lunch in your office we expected, but what about this surprise you promised? A honey blintz for dessert? I don't think so."

"Well, feast your eyes then." Hammond dimmed the lights and scrolled down on his laptop to the folder with the slides Phyllis Farber had given him. He turned on the overhead projector to screen the slide of the back of the panel Farber said she was keeping in her office safe. He zoomed in for a close-up, then out again. "I thought you'd like starting with this, Dara; it's a treat for you lab types."

"You mean because, yes, it looks like the real thing? At first sight anyway."

"Say more."

"Zoom in and out again, slowly this time. Let's see. Old wood, a little smoky-colored, scorched on the bottom edge but not obviously messed with or made up, except for the reinforcements someone screwed on, probably a long time ago. As much warping as you'd expect; some nice wiggly worm holes that nails or knitting needles can't fake. It's made out of three vertical boards, cut with the grain, probably poplar; the kind of wood you start to see a little after 1300. No owner's marks or inventory numbers. That's a little suspicious; could be that they were wiped away at some point. Or that it's just an old door someone cut up."

Malcolm Sargeant broke in. "Good to know that, I'm sure, Dara, but I don't do wood without paint on it. Am I just imagining that there's color on the other side?"

Hammond scrolled to the next slide and waited for Malcolm to take it in.

"Red flags. I mean have you actually seen this, Jeremy?"

"I tried, but it's pretty clear that Farber's going to keep it under wraps until she gets the opinions she wants. And Satterby's is going along with that."

"That figures. Dealers not liking surprises unless they produce them. But our good friend Phyllis must have said something about it."

"She did say that it's unpublished…"

Malcolm snorted. "No doubt about that."

"…sketchy provenance, attributed to Giotto."

"Three strikes, in other words. Four if you count"—Malcolm made a clicking sound—"the Venetian 'Giotto' that people are all excited about without having seen it. They're calling it San Maurizio; so we're supposed to believe that not just one but two Giotto warrior saints have popped up all at once. As Dara says, I don't think so."

"Well, I don't know," Dara adopted the needling tone with which she and Malcolm enjoyed provoking one another. "Strange things do happen, even in this solemn temple of art. Like our pictures getting reattributed from time to time. The last time I heard the count was about 80%. Better than Atlantic City odds, I'll admit."

"So no one's going to bet on this 'Giotto.'"

"Don't be so sure, Malcolm. The front office isn't going sit back and watch it get picked off by the Getty or sheiks somewhere. But, seriously, the provenance thing may not matter so much. Go figure. A tiny Madonna, supposedly from 14th-century Siena, supposedly by Duccio, turns up after

700 years in a Russian collection as quickly as you can say Beef Stroganoff; it reappears at Christie's out of the blue to be bought by us for a huge price, total amount undisclosed. A Madonna and Child like it suddenly turns up in London, goes missing in a Geneva bank vault, pops up after thirty years."

"Come on, Dara. You haven't given us the punchline: we forget a few messy details and get a little Madonna with *Duccio di Buoninsegna* on its caption."

"Anyway," Malcolm went on, "we weren't working for this august institution ten years ago. And we're looking at these photos of a picture now. Giotto-like—at least. Black warrior saint with sword and spear, possible props for San Maurizio. More of him in blackface after 1500; some black medieval ones too. But a saint with company on one panel—not likely until, say, a century after Giotto's time. It's the kind of pastiche, mix and match, that trips up forgers."

Hammond tried turning the tables on Malcolm. "Unless only a Giotto could have done such an amazing thing. Making Crusader miniatures from the East into Latin pictures in the West. Our front office had to rewrite the history of Western art to put their pricey Duccio Madonna in the top tier. So they could do that for this picture."

Dara put on a solemn face. "Ah yes, Dr. Hammond, that embarrassing prose about Duccio being Matisse to Giotto's Picasso. Some rewriting for a black Giotto saint would be inspirational. Multicultural, very political correct just now. Definitely possible."

"Assuming that you can make the technical stuff look plausible."

"Did Farber say anything about that?"

"She did say she didn't have an electron microscope handy."

"Her little jab. Meaning that the lab spoils too many sales."

"Unless the sales and the joke are on the lab when you experts don't agree and there's big money riding on the opinion the market wants. Farber knows the ropes."

Dara nodded. "She's done her own basic light show, I suppose. To head us off."

"Of course. You can see some of it in the next slides. Not too much scraping or overpainting under strong light; lots of old varnish—green and yellow under ultraviolet; black underdrawing and the faces in infrared. I don't know that they did all that much on our alleged Duccio back at Christie's in London."

"Why would they? Our exquisitely discerning connoisseurs judged it to be for real and for the ages. The baby's thrilling, tender touch; a human revolution in art. Grubby lab philistines and archive boors need not apply."

"You know, Farber did say something about archives. The document a John Terterian student found in Venice. Pretty reliable evidence, she says, that Enrico Scrovegni donated a painting of San Maurizio to the saint's church in Venice. It would be like old Scrovegni to spare nothing to get Giotto back to work for him. Why not?"

***

Phyllis Farber clearly wanted a good return from sending him off with slides of "her" picture. Jeremy Hammond had no illusions about that. She meant to use him; she already had done so by dropping his name to the arts editor at the *Times*. A reporter had called him about a St. Mauritius picture in New York. He had hedged.

Farber could be just testing him with a fake to see if he could tell the difference. It wouldn't be the first time she had used the trip-up-an-expert gambit. But Dara and Malcolm had given him some reassurance about the picture. Maybe Farber supposed she could manipulate him as an up-and-coming newcomer at the Met. Getting him on record before making her pitch to the higher-ups. Hammond had no illusions about that, either. The museum was as hierarchical as the army or the church. His best guess was that he was her designated trial balloon or, if she needed to back off, a sacrificial lamb. He could go along with that, the balloon part anyway.

She wasn't going to give him much time to mull it over in any case. She had made light of setting deadlines, but then scheduled an appointment at her office in a few days' time. He was efficient when he had to be, but a procrastinator by choice. He decided he would tell her about his conversation with Dara and Malcolm. She could make what she wanted of it.

Walking down Madison Avenue toward the appointment, he window shopped the lineup of glitzy boutiques without much interest; luxury bait was pretty much the same anywhere. At 75th Street he looked with a resigned shrug at Marcel Breuer's Whitney Museum. The upside down ziggurat had outlived critical slurs on the way to becoming everybody's icon of mid-20th-century modernism. Now, with the Whitney moving downtown to another celebrity architect's showplace, the Met was going to colonize the old Whitney's stack of cement blocks for its imperial move into modern art. Satterby's headquarters three blocks further down was just another New York glass box pretending that its business was transparent.

"Very interesting, Jeremy," Farber had said of his exchange with Dara and Malcolm. "Some people would go out on a limb with that report. Art does that to people, doesn't it? Where we be otherwise? Of course at the Met you need to be more careful, or give the impression of being so."

Hammond waited for whatever was coming next. "That's why they're taking so much time with your 16th-century German St. Moritz, keeping quiet about it for years now. They got burned by rushing for the little Duccio Madonna, if that's what it is. Not that they'll ever admit it."

So the old girl already knew about a third picture of "her" saint. Hammond had been told that the Cranach panel was an in-house secret, in the conservation lab for now. He shifted from alarm to relief that he was not the source of the leak.

Farber gauged his reaction, then went on. "But of course the German picture can't compete with my Giotto."

"Are you sure?" Hammond was not sure of much of anything at that point, but had composed himself enough to ask the question.

"Shouldn't I be?"

"Too many pictures of the same subject showing up in too many places all at once. Suspicious. Flooding the market."

"More likely attracting interest, splashy headlines, adding value."

"Maybe so, Phyllis. But I can see you why you're not worried about the competition. Pictures of a black St. Moritz from Germany aren't all that rare; the best ones were done long after Giotto's time; they're mostly humdrum. Grünewald's overgrown black toy soldier in Munich is wonderful, but old Cranach and his workshop churned out pattern book black Moritizes, at least two of them besides the one you seem to know we've got at the Met. Funny to think of the Germans being so politically correct."

"So you agree, Jeremy. The German picture just makes mine look better."

"Well, Cranach did dress the saint up as a pretty boy in a floppy red hat with white feather trim and glittery fashion-plate armor. But he's no Giotto, if that's what you mean." Hammond left it that. He had quite enough of saint what's-his-name for the day.

***

After the session at Satterby's Jeremy Hammond felt he deserved a break and took the Lexington Express downtown. He had found an apartment on 16th Street at 3d Avenue. It was a pleasantly old-fashioned enclave of a neighborhood, with a little park at the end of the block, a Victorian pile of a church on one side of 16th Street and a Quaker school founded in 1786 on the other. The apartment looked out to the Empire State and the Chrysler buildings, not a plutocrat's view but, from the fourteenth floor, high enough. It was conveniently close to Union Square and protectively distant from the Museum Mile.

The reliably courteous greeting from one of the Latino doormen was like a blessing for a quiet late afternoon. Hammond took the elevator to his floor, ready to settle down with a glass of a favorite Italian Alto Adige white. He was feeling just guilty enough not to ignore the ping of a message on his phone. It was a text from Letizia Bassani, with mock headlines:

"How Will Dr. Jeremy Hammond Come Down on S. Maurizio? All Venice Hopes He Will Not Betray Us." She added a P.S. "We need to talk."

Letizia was one of Jeremy Hammond's best friends from his dissertation days in Venice. He was analyzing the painting cycle in one of the Venetian *scuole*, the confraternities where second-class citizens in the tight social hierarchy could outdo their patrician betters by commissioning great works of art. Letizia was working upscale from Jeremy on patrician art patrons. They had debated one another's regrettable choices over many a glass in a favorite wine bar near the archive but called it a draw when Letizia had landed a job at the Accademia gallery about the same time Jeremy was hired at the Met.

They had toasted this double feat the last time Jeremy was in Venice. Rolling a wine glass between her fingers, Letizia said in that Italian way of speaking about Italy as a distant and disreputable foreign country, "You know what the Italian Economic Miracle is these days. Having any job at all. Doesn't matter what you're trained for; depends on who you know. The Italians are still courtiers, licking ass or having their relatives do it. And even then…"

"Anyway, *cara*, everyone knows you're deserving."

"So what favors are you after from me, Jeremy?" They had a good laugh as he lifted her hand for a theatrical kiss.

It was like Letizia "to make a scene," as his mother would have said. He decided to call her back right away, partly to fend off lingering thoughts of maternal disapproval. It would be late morning in Venice now. Letizia answered on the first ring. "You've got us in an uproar here, you know."

The usual state of affairs in Italy, Hammond thought. *Not that anything ever changes because of that.*

She hurried on. "Everybody's saying it must be a fake, that New York picture in your *Times* quote; or if it's not, everybody wants it back. Point of national honor, meaning Venetian honor of course. Brambilla's got a pass for now. Some *pezzi grossi*—'bigshots,' you say?—want us to go after him; so far he's untouchable. But we've had a sudden twitch of duty about regulations on exported national treasures or looted ones. And Giotto—a very Big Deal.

Hammond waited for her to wind down. "Who's 'everybody,' Letizia?"

She hesitated. "Well, you know…"

He did know. *Tutto il mondo*, "the whole world," often best translated as "your family, your school friends, your workmates."

"Have you talked to Regina Payne? She's seen both pictures just recently and she's the one who found the Scrovegni document about one or the other—or neither—of them."

"I haven't actually. But everybody knows whose side she's going to take."

6

Regina had been away for just a little more than a week, but that was time enough for a quick Vivaldi tempo change of season. The air had shifted from heavy luxuriance to a spare chill with episodes of rain or fog. Everything looked thinner, even the crowds. Colors paled to resentful imitations of themselves or disappeared altogether. Regina hadn't realized quite so fully before that the great Venetian painters had mostly stopped time in spring or summer. The terra cotta tiles that were cooling in hot weather chilled her to the bone. Her wool blanket and fleecy quilt were cold comfort after Milan.

Giovanni had asked her to stay with him there just as she was leaving for New York. She was uneasy about it. It sounded like he expected her to come to him. As if it were for him to decide that they would go on seeing one another. The heroine in a trashy novel would "throw caution to the wind" and "fly into the arms of her lover." And inevitably come to regret it. That might happen, but Regina had taken her chances on the way back from New York. She wanted to believe that he was interested in more than the novelty of bedding a black American historian of art; it wouldn't necessarily be unpleasant if she were wrong.

He had shown her a few sights in Milan. That was a good start. He talked a little about his game: the speed; the teammates he liked; the thrill of a goal, especially when it rubbed the jeering fans of the other team the wrong way. Until she met him she wouldn't have cared, but it was intriguing now to catch a glimpse of a world, his world, she knew nothing about. She liked his way of saying just enough without presuming that she was dying to know more. He wasn't stuck on himself. He had asked for the latest news about her adventures with Giotto and San Maurizio. His penthouse apartment was a glass pleasure dome and they had made appropriate use of it through a long night.

The next morning she took her turn in cutting their time together short. It was probably best that way; not to press Giovanni—or herself—to come to terms just then with their relationship. Besides, she had promised Terterian, after being remiss before, that she would be following up leads in Venice. The understanding before she left that she and Giovanni would see one another soon eased the leave-taking.

Back in Venice, she huddled for warmth in bed with coffee and her iPad. She was behind on the news. Passing over the daily fare of crises and failed solutions, she scrolled to the Arts Section of the *New York Times*. She never expected much from art world chatter—an interesting story sometimes, often comic relief from expressions of shock about the latest scandal—but this time the lead headline pulled her up short: *Giotto in Black and White?*

The story began with "a spectacular discovery": a previously unknown painting attributed to Giotto had turned up in New York. "If the painting can be authenticated," the reporter wrote, as if that were already a sure thing, "it would force a rethinking of the canon of Western art history." The article went on to cite "the respected dealer in Old Masters Phyllis Farber." She was quoted as saying, "We've had many modern masters come to market lately, but it's exceedingly rare to have anything come to light by an early Renaissance master, indeed the founding father of Renaissance painting, and anything so unique as the subject of this panel."

A curator of early European painting at the Met, Jeremy Hammond, offered a "cautious but positive opinion": "A black warrior-saint from the 14th century—it's certainly unusual but not impossible. The early Christian martyr St. Mauritius, if it is him, was often represented as black in Western art." As for the attribution to Giotto, the article continued, that would doubtless be controversial. "But," Hammond had added, "few hard facts are known about him; we do know of course that he was a pioneer, inventive ahead of his time, but it is too soon to say much more until the picture is thoroughly tested and examined, and more is known about its provenance."

The reporter saved an "astonishing coincidence" for the punch line. There were rumors, so far unconfirmed, that a similar painting had surfaced in Venice, with the difference that the figures in that version were evidently white men. Little was known about it so far. The owner was said to be Piergiorgio Brambilla, a Milanese financier with a palace on the Grand Canal, but he had not responded so far to requests for comment. The reporter capped off the story with a flourish about a forthcoming duel between two rival saints, white and black, and the inevitable speculations about the tens, even hundreds of millions of dollars a Giotto original would bring.

***

The *Gazettino* was quick to pick up the *New York Times* story. It was hometown news, not just one more tedious report about endless crises in Rome or some irrelevant catastrophe in the faraway world outside Venice. The prospect of interminable controversies and investigations promised reams of good copy, inevitably so in Italy.

Gasparo Corner was, as always, trolling for a back story. "Everybody's talking about it, Piergiorgio," he had said quietly over a drink with Brambilla as if the regulars at the Gritti Palace bar had to be kept from hearing what they already knew. "Even on the Accademia bridge on my way here." Then practically in a whisper, "They say that there are going to be official inquiries. But that won't involve you, will it?"

"I'm sure the authorities have better things to do," said Brambilla in a voice meant to be heard. He did not give the slightest hint that he had arranged for the rumors about the story to be leaked, knowing that it would create a tantalizing sensation in the art world and the press. It would build up suspense; it would increase support for his plans in the saint's neighborhood. And it would likely bring the opposition to whatever he was doing out in the open where he could deal with it.

"Yes, of course, Piergiorgio. But unfortunately we are so rich in scandals that our overburdened forces of law and order must pick and choose. It's a *casinò*. Worse than playing the gambling tables at the Palazzo Vendramin."

And, it went without saying, no less rigged. Brambilla knew without looking that heads were nodding agreement around the room. It didn't take long for conspiracy theories to spread and bets to be cast on the outcome.

Brambilla's friend Paolo Michiel in the Prosecutors office had already clued him in.

"The Consorzio's Big Project gang is pretty desperate. No surprise about that, with all the indictments raining down. It's like we're on the devil's ladder, going down and down. His Excellency the Mayor; the Godfather of it all, Engineer Mazzacessi; a couple of regional councilors on the take; Codarelli from the environmental ministry in Rome."

Brambilla feigned astonishment. "Thirty-four, I hear."

"Still counting. The thing is we've cracked the system open this time. The way funds from Rome, the Region, City Hall get siphoned off from bogus accounting: estimates, cost overruns, you name it. That's what kept the whole show going."

"But you knew that all along, Paolo."

Michiel shrugged off the flattery as well as the implicit blame. "That was before we could put all the pieces together. Indict someone and others would take over somewhere else, out of reach. They'd string it out, but the double dealing isn't working this time, even in Italy."

"Even in Venice?"

"Well, it's not going to play out easily for them. They're flailing around, looking for other targets. Scapegoats. When somebody can't be bought off, that's when the things get serious, turn rough. You can't be bought off, so they've got you in their sights, Piergiorgio."

"Same old stuff no doubt. I'm a *foresto*, an outsider; worse, Milanese. Meddling. Lording it over pathetic little Campo San Maurizio. Turning up my nose at the really serious plans for the lagoon. Insult on top of injury, partial to those black monkeys on the calcio field, probably paying off the referees too. That's old stuff, Paolo."

Michiel didn't bother to look surprised. Brambilla never missed much. "Yes, old stuff, but it's got heavier, you know. They've still got cronies, sympathizers anyway, people in high places—all beyond suspicion of course. Enough to put you on trial in the papers, deny permits, string out 'necessary investigations.' They can get tough, call in the ultras, give them political cover as true patriots of San Marco. This story about the paintings, they're going to make a big deal of it."

"Loving art as they do."

"On their honor, with all sincerity. Whatever the museum people, the Soprintendenza, the Carabinieri, the NGOs, the magistrates want to hear. They'll demand answers. Where your picture came from; whether it's the real thing; why Giovanni Bonelli is hanging out with that black trick of a woman who has supposedly got something on the picture."

"And," Brambilla surmised, "why I'm not taking on the Americans and proclaiming from the rooftops that their picture is stolen or fake. White over Black, Venetian honor at stake."

***

"*Ciao, cara*," Flavia had texted. "What's going on with you and those trickster guys? Magnate, Saint, Chick Bait. For me, I'm doing the clown for carnival, Arlecchino."

Regina covered her annoyance with a carnival jibe. "Not the Plague Doctor with the long pointy nose?" She knew perfectly well what Flavia meant but didn't want to acknowledge it. Some strain of American confidence—or was it innocence?—persisted no matter what. In Italy confidence usually came from being cynical. That's Flavia, "doing Arlecchino." But for better or worse, clowns were often truth tellers.

On second thought, Regina wasn't going to jump to conclusions. Maybe that was American too; the Italian way was being quick to judge, usually to blame, and slow to forget. Giovanni had asked at the reception if she wanted to be introduced to Brambilla; he hadn't pressed it. Cinderella that she was, it was fitting that she should meet her host in the palace. She was introduced after Brambilla had given his little speech about plans for his neighborhood; so it was not out of line for her to mention her research or for the great man to be interested. She hadn't made a secret of it. She could have been more careful, but she was caught up in a headlong chase and excited that someone outside the art world would care. And after hearing Brambilla inviting her to meet with him, why wouldn't Giovanni be interested in knowing the score?

He had emailed that he wanted to come to Venice. To be with her, he said. He could borrow a launch and meet her at the Guglie bridge to make some carnival rounds from there if she liked. There was going to be a masked ball at the Palazzo Bastagli, but they wouldn't have to do the VIP thing. His friend had offered him the apartment again. No rooms of state; just elegant and, she might remember, intimate.

Regina wasn't sure about the carnival part. From old paintings she knew that the Venetians liked dress-ups and revels. And, from the web, that the tourist trade had reinvented carnival as a come-on: Venice as Carnival Fun City again. Just the thing to bring in the crowds when tourism was slow in the winter months. Never mind that there were already enough carnival stands and mask shops in all seasons to sink the city if *acqua alta* didn't do it first. But it *was* carnival season after all, not just for the tourists and not a good time for serious reality checks. If Giovanni was stringing her along, she would enjoy it while she could; Flavia wouldn't have hesitated for a minute.

She didn't regret her decision when he bounded from the polished boat deck onto the Fondamenta of the Cannaregio Canal. It would have been a winning move on the playing field. She gave herself over to his embrace. She had missed him, probably more than she should have.

It was already dark on the short winter day. The bright lanterns on the bridge illuminated the scene like a movie set. Some passers-by recognized Giovanni as Regina eased her way out of his arms. Three tough looking guys were not dressed up for carnival but their skinhead look and bomber jackets looked like costumes. One of them hooted, "We'll see you later, asshole fucking Gianni boy."

Regina pulled Giovanni towards some of the ubiquitous mask stands. "Wearing one of those we won't be bothered." They bought a couple of masks from the vendor who promised his best price if he could take a selfie with Giovanni.

It turned out that ambling around in the crowd was more fun than being snobbish about it. In their masks Giovanni and Regina were anonymous, not just because they were disguised but because carnival masks were mostly variations on a few traditional types. They had picked the plain white *volto* that covered the face, but so had many other people. "Liberation for sale," Flavia had called the vendors' masks, "mostly made in China. A sack over your head would be more creative."

There were sideshows on the bridges and in almost every campo. Rowdy students and reeling Brits were making hard work of having a good time; kids played hide-and-seek; singing was on offer in a choice of tunes and languages. The crowd's current flowed toward Piazza San Marco, which was decked out for carnival like an overgrown burlesque theater. The evening's costume contest featured gaudy purple, pink, ultramarine colors and flashes of fake metal. Disembodied heads sported turbans with horns; hats like lampshades or towers glided like miniature carnival floats. Regina had seen rows of costumes for rent by the hour in a shop window. It occurred to her that the elaborate processionals art historians took so seriously in Renaissance paintings probably seemed at least a little campy in their own time.

After the noisy crowd and thumping music, Regina was more than ready to move on. She had heard about the Metropole's "Dinner with Casanova" and more exclusive entertainments for the jet set. She wondered whether Giovanni was still thinking about the masked ball at Brambilla's, but he said he really wanted time with her alone. "You won't be surprised by that, will you?"

With an arm around her shoulders, he guided her toward the west portico that Napoleon had built to close off the Piazza San Marco and seal the doom of the republic. Once through the arcade and across the junction of Calle Frezzeria and Calle Vallaresso, the crowd broke into small groups looking for the next party. The church of San Moise, Moses baptized as a Christian saint, loomed up like an oversized carnival confection. Regina got her bearings after a warren of dead-end passageways when they turned into another campo with a branch leading to the Giglio vaporetto stop. "We're getting close to Brambilla's palazzo," she said. "I thought we weren't going to be VIPs tonight."

"We're not. Just to the apartment. We'll salute San Maurizio's Campo. We owe him; he's how we met. You won't miss your cold bed in Cannaregio tonight, will you?"

She would not, but before she said so, Giovanni looked back abruptly over his shoulder, then quickened the pace. "I think those guys have been following us, the ones from the bridge." He grabbed Regina's hand and, almost running, steered her toward the green door of the apartment on the edge of the Campo. Without looking back he pulled a key out of his pocket, gave the lock a quick double twist, pulled Regina inside, and slammed the door shut. Moments later there was a loud banging on the door.

"So you're out on the town, Gianni boy. Playing games, masks and all. Monkey Boy, Black Bitch all the same." More pounding, laughing, bottles crashing on the door. "Just wait til next time, you and the *puttana*."

It happened so fast that Regina didn't realize how frightened she was until the noise receded. She clung to Giovanni, shaking. "What was that about?" she whispered.

Giovanni held her close. "Maybe they're jealous of my hanging out with you."

Regina was not going to be put off. "But they wouldn't know or care who I am."

"Name in the papers, smell of scandal. Venetians live for stuff like that. They're bored by what goes on outside the lagoon. Don't worry. We'll be fine here. Come on, let's go up. Remember? The elevator actually works."

The apartment was just as enchanting as she remembered. Even better after the scare they'd had. "Another miracle," Regina said. "San Maurizio's saved us. Your friend too."

"He'd like to hear that."

Regina looked up sharply. "Brambilla. Of course. It's him." She nodded with a gesture of indignation that would have passed well enough for an Italian's. "This is his deal." She raised her voice. "It's his place, his model apartment. Just around the corner from his palazzo. I see. He wants something from me. And you're going along with him."

"Wait a minute, Regina. It's not like that. There are big shots who have it in for him, for me too. They've got their eyes on you…"

"That's ridiculous. What's that got to do with me?"

"They've seen us together; they've been spying on Brambilla. Look, Regina, you don't know what these guys are like. They're targeting people they think got them in trouble with their homegrown mafia on the lagoon. Recruiting toughs like those guys, skinheads and crazies all fired up to 'liberate' Venice. They're sure Brambilla's out to get them. They can't understand why we would be paying attention to you unless it's some kind of plot and you're getting paid off."

Regina had to laugh in spite of herself. "Student art historian. I'd come pretty cheap."

He wasn't listening. "They figure they can get something on him through that picture of his—that it's stolen, illegal—something like that; that he's going to ship it out of the country; that he's making big bets on it. Anything like that to tangle him up in the law; the way we do it here. For years. Maybe to get him out of Venice that way, to lick his wounds, mind his own business."

"If it's really like that," Regina cried, "he can take care of himself. Isn't that what he always does?" Her outrage subsided with her struggle to think about what it all meant. "So what I am supposed to do?" she finally said more calmly than she felt.

"Forgive me for making trouble for you. Let me make it up to you tonight. Or longer." Giovanni put his arms around her gently. She couldn't bring herself to resist.

***

Regina stretched in the luxury of smooth linen and soft down, willfully ignoring decisions she had to face. She reached over to Giovanni for reassurance. Startled by the feel of cool bedding, she sat up quickly, then sank back with relief to the sound of dishes and the perfume of coffee.

"Another surprise, good this time," she said smiling as Giovanni entered the bedroom with a tray and bent down to kiss her. He stroked her cheek, hesitated, then stood up. "I'm sorry about the next one—surprise, I mean. I have to go to Milan."

"You *have* to go… Again," she heard herself saying. Then coldly, "And you just forgot to tell me…"

"When you were so upset? It won't be very long and you can stay here."

"After what happened last night?"

"Look, Regina, I understand. But you'll be alright here. Those guys last night, they're just paid toughs. The big shots will figure they got the message sent. They'll wait and see what happens. They've got other things to worry about. Brambilla does too." Giovanni drew her close. "It'll be just a few days and you'll be safe here."

She wavered. He might be right. But why should she trust him now?

***

I have to think about it. Regina repeated the mantra over and over as she took the elevator down, opened the door, turned and passed San Maurizio, its façade benignly camouflaged by fog. She had decided to take a roundabout walk through Cannaregio to her apartment. To give herself time to think or, as happens in Venice, to be distracted.

The swirling fog played tricks, but Regina's building was exempt from any misty magic. The flickering neon and seawater-mildew smell wafting up the stairwell were perfectly familiar, even a little reassuring after the stagey remodel.

Or so it seemed until, climbing the stairs, she sensed that something was wrong. She stopped to listen, then continued as quietly as she could. At her landing she saw that her door was ajar. She didn't think she could have left it open; even if she had, her obsessive landlady would have locked it and left a stern reprimand behind.

She eased the door open. At first it didn't seem that anything was the matter. Two chairs by the table were askew. Nothing particularly unusual about that. Opening the door further, she saw that the portable TV was still there; so was her spare purse. She straightened the chairs as she crossed towards the little room where she had set up a makeshift study.

"Oh my god!" she gasped. The floor was strewn with books and papers. The work table had been turned over; a milk crate with files of notes, photos, and clippings had been emptied out and rifled. Her laptop was gone.

Shocked, frightened, angry, she sat down on the empty crate to steady herself. Paranoia was an occupational hazard for researchers—people looking over your shoulders at your notes or accusing someone of stealing their material. But paranoids have real enemies, and it was becoming clearer all the time that she had company in her obsession with San Maurizio. Brambilla and whoever had broken in. And that wasn't even counting New York.

And what about Giovanni? A one night stand, then off somewhere the next morning. Taking her for granted? Other women? Regina wasn't going to slink back to the fancy apartment and wait. Wait for what? For Giovanni when she couldn't trust him; for those thugs who probably could be trusted to make more trouble; for Brambilla to make contact. Bad scenarios, all of them.

She texted Flavia: "Can you come to my apartment? Something bad's happened."

"You can't stay here," Flavia declared surveying the damage. It was her free early morning and she had rushed over. "Get some things together. You can stay at my place until we figure out what to do. You're not going to wait around for them to come again. If you call the police, they'll just tell you to keep your door locked even if you already did it three times."

7

Jeremy Hammond in New York and Letizia Bassani in Venice were exchanging texts for light relief from what had become serious business for them both. He started it by asking playfully which of them was going to get in bigger trouble over the San Maurizio affair. "You've got a head start," she shot back, "with the big splash you made in the *Times*." She didn't mention that she had been assigned to find out what she could, so long as it was incriminating, about the Brambilla picture.

"Not fair, Letizia. I was just rolling with Phyllis Farber's power lunches. Anyway Maurizio's supposed to protect martyrs in case we need him."

After their last lunch Farber had shopped her campaign for a Maurizio show at the Met. She already had her lines down pat for "this splendid opportunity."

"I call it," she said as if the show were a done deal, "Two Masterpieces of a Black Saint Rediscovered: Diversity and Tolerance in the Canon of Renaissance Art." The Museum would show its Cranach together with "her" Giotto on loan: "Multicultural Icons from the Very Beginning of the Renaissance in Italy through the Golden Age of German Art."

Hammond waited for what he knew was coming. "Of course you'll want to be on board, Jeremy."

"I thought I left plenty of wiggle room in the *Times*." He hoped he sounded sure of himself. He didn't mention what she already knew and disregarded; that it was supposed to be out of bounds for the Museum to tout a dealer's goods. "More study needed and all that. Anyway no one was talking then about hanging it in a big show."

"Ah, but that was before the *Times* piece. There's all the fallout since then."

"Just the usual chatter."

"Do you really believe that, Jeremy?"

He did, partly. The Museum's response had been officious and more than a little dismissive. "Dr. Hammond was not speaking officially in the *Times* of course"; "you will understand that our painstaking research and exacting treatment of works of art cannot be rushed." This museumspeak practically invited predictable criticism for "insensitivity, elitism, and a lack of transparency."

Farber had a different take. "It wasn't just chatter that you sounded out your colleagues before talking to the *Times*."

"You know that."

"But not everybody does. And as for the Venice picture, it wouldn't be kept under cover unless there's something seriously wrong with it. Who knows where it came from? My clients assure me they can account for theirs. Our Giotto's looking better all the time."

Hammond translated to himself: *On with the show.*

***

Letizia Bassani's assignment to the Brambilla Case, as it was being called now, had come as a surprise. The Director of the Accademia had summoned her to his office without specifying a reason. There was nothing out of the ordinary about an arbitrary summons. The company of beautiful things did not necessarily refine the manners of museum officials. What was different was the unusually cordial greeting. The Director rose from his bureaucrat's desk and conducted Letizia to the elegantly furnished private study off to one side.

"I hope you have found your work rewarding in your few months with us, dottoressa," he said, inviting her to sit opposite him in one of the tapestried side chairs that would have graced a museum exhibit and probably had. Since this actually sounded like a question, not a directive, Bassani answered positively enough without seeming either too eager or too reserved.

The Director nodded approvingly. "I think you might find it especially interesting to undertake a special research project for us; that is, for the Accademia and the Soprintendenza. You see, dottoressa, we are collaborating in an important investigation."

Something else unusual: the museum and the agency regulating all the fine arts in Venice were often at odds in bureaucratic infighting.

"The investigation calls for someone with your outstanding scholarly credentials." Letizia waited for him to get past the flattering touches to the qualifications that mattered. "And in particular someone who knows the city intimately and would be, shall we say, discreet, inconspicuous, beyond suspicion." In the endless project of unifying the country and discouraging corruption, the bureaucrats and the police were regularly, less often rationally, transferred from one region to another. It was certainly the case that the Director's Roman manner made him conspicuously foreign to anyone north of Chioggia or south of Treviso. Bassani knew that his "inconspicuous" probably meant being expendable if someone had to be blamed.

The Director adjusted his cuffs, good form for continuing in an orderly manner. "I trust that you have been attentive to the reports circulating about recently discovered works attributed to Giotto, one of them here in Venice in the possession of Piergiorgio Brambilla."

No answer was required or expected this time. "These reports raise many questions." Again a pause for a gratuitous appeal for discretion. "Among many other concerns, we have been given to understand by credible sources that the painting was illicitly obtained; therefore that Piergiorgio Brambilla cannot be the rightful owner and indeed may be subject to prosecution."

"You will understand that this is a delicate matter." What that usually meant was it would be forgotten unless, as Letizia understood perfectly well, powerful pressures were being exerted to the contrary.

"Therefore, we must proceed with cautious deliberation. We do not want to alert Commendatore Brambilla; and until we can connect the dots, as they say, we do not want the police and the magistrates to engage prematurely in some unfortunate, no doubt clumsy inquiry. The staff will be informed that you have been assigned half time to a research project."

"With a deadline?" Bassani asked, wary of half-time likely taking all her time.

"That depends on you; that is, on the results. But you will appreciate that we want your findings as soon as possible."

Letizia Bassani smiled as if in agreement but actually because she was amused by his "as soon as possible." It probably hadn't occurred to the Director that he could have done much of the research more efficiently and more confidentially himself.

The databases of the Art Theft Division of the Carabinieri and Interpol or NGOs like the Art Recovery Group were on line. She had already made a quick check when the papers started reporting about the "sensational simultaneous appearance of hitherto unknown images of San Maurizio." The "unknown" part was correct so far as she could tell; lost or stolen pictures possibly corresponding to either picture were not listed. She had no trouble locating a serious monograph on representations of the saint in the Cini Foundation library at San Giorgio. There were a few promising links amidst the dross on the Internet. She wondered how much more Regina Payne already knew.

***

In her campaign for a Met show Phyllis Farber kept John Terterian on tap. She called him when she read that he was going to be in New York for a lecture at the New School. She flinched at the title: "Deconstructing Mimesis: Trans- and Cis-sexted Bodies in Renaissance Art."

"I'm sure you're not calling about the lecture, Phyllis. The graduate students suggested it, but I'll let you in on a secret. The title is bait for springing some close looking at pictures on them."

"How bad of you, John. Shocking them that way. If you can get away unscathed, I hope you'll have time to talk about the list of Giotto scholars I asked you about."

"You must have your own list by now."

"Yes, but you can help me tweak it."

Terterian might have begged off, but he was too involved for that with the mystery, intrigue, scandal, or whatever this Maurizio affair turned out to be. And there was Regina to consider. When he said he wouldn't have much time, with a train to catch after the lecture, Farber hadn't skipped a beat and proposed that they meet at the Campbell Apartment bar, a Twenties railway tycoon's hideaway right inside Grand Central Station.

The New School was close to Union Square and it was only one stop from there by the 4 or 5 subway express to Grand Central. Almost everything was grandiose in that monument of the heroic age of capitalism, but not the side door to the Campbell Apartment. It was set at an odd angle near the exit to the incongruous slice of Vanderbilt Avenue on the east side of the station. The door opened into a vestibule with a small stairway rising toward a red plush curtain. Terterian drew it aside to look around a room of faux medieval wood paneling and stained glass. Farber signaled from one of the niches in the mezzanine.

"You'll be safe here from your students, John," she quipped while making room for him.

"Actually they were quite interested, excited even. Looking at Rosso Fiorentino and Pontormo does that to people."

"I hope it won't be too boring to go from mannerist maniacs to Giotto."

"Your list. Of Giotto scholars. Preferably some you can count on. That's a hard order to fill, as you know."

She looked at him steadily over the rim of her glass. "That's why I asked you."

Terterian left the invitation to conspiracy hanging. "A friend I've known since graduate school—he's been trying for years to sort out the Giotto from the non-Giotto frescoes in Assisi—told me when I saw him last, 'We're a picky bunch'—he meant Giotto scholars—'because we have so little to go on and there are fewer and fewer of us these days.'"

"How am I supposed to interpret that?" Phyllis fingered her pearls before answering her own question. "It could mean that we can pick and choose since the experts are certain to differ with one another."

"You might do that if you're prepared to go to court for it. With experts on both sides and lawyers on all sides suing for damages."

"But they have to prove willful negligence. That's a high bar and there's always the escape clause: *Satterby's is not liable for changes in attribution.*"

"So you can't get blamed for the latest up-and-down count of real Rembrandts—or Giottos. But two Giottos coming out of nowhere at the same time. It's a stretch."

Phyllis raised her glass as if for a toast. "Not if we bait and switch. Look at it this way, John. Your Regina's Scrovegni hook could work for both pictures. But ours is the right color. If a black San Maurizio was good enough for the old emperors, it's good enough for anybody. Besides no one seems to know where Brambilla's picture came from. Anyway my sources are telling me that he's not interested in selling; that it's going to the saint's church in Venice. A ploy, bribe, gift? Brambilla fancying himself a modern day Scrovegni? Who knows? The point is that the way is open for my picture. To put it on loan for a big Met show, and if they don't take it for a record price, Abu Dhabi or some unspeakably rich collector will."

***

"Do you have a lunch surprise for us again, Jeremy?" Dara Levy surveyed the brown bags on Jeremy Hammond's work table at the Met. "I don't think it's a gourmet treat."

"I didn't have someone on an expense account to pick up the tab."

Malcolm Sargeant responded with a quick tilt of his head. "Like Phyllis Farber, you mean. She seems to have taken a special fancy to you, Jeremy. Those dreamy blue eyes, the Brit look. Certainly not just business as usual. It couldn't be that she wants anything from humble servants of art like Dara and me."

It wasn't clear whether Dara was rolling her eyes at Jeremy or Malcolm or both. "Come on, gentlemen, let's see what's for lunch; then we'll do the update that we know we're here for. It's not polite talk with your mouth full. Please pass the corned beef and rye and the apple juice."

There were a couple of hard copies of *The Art Newspaper* on the table, slumming it with the *Daily News*. Dara rifled through the *Daily News* with one hand for her daily scandal fix. The *Art Newspaper,* much quicker on the draw since it had gone on line, had picked up early on reports about the alleged Giotto pictures. Old pictures weren't news for the tabloids, but the rumor that one of them showed a black man, a warrior saint no less, was bound to sell papers.

"We haven't we seen you quoted in the *Times* lately, Jeremy." Malcolm said, pushing aside the remains of his sandwich and reaching for the coffee. "With all the scuttlebutt about Phyllis's latest 'sensational plan' she must be looking for some quotes again."

Dara piped in. "For a kind of a double header, it sounds like. She probably can probably get an OK for our German St. Moritz. It's finally out of conservation. Research is pretty much done too. Old Cranach doing a pretty boy black saint for a fat German archbishop, the one who ticked off Luther; he was a kleptomaniac about church offices and relics. A whiff of scandal's always a draw for a show."

Jeremy looked up from having busied himself with the clean up. "So what am I going to say now about Phyllis's 'Giotto'?" He drew quotes in the air around the name. "I guess it's no secret that I'm supposed to research what our front office should think about it."

"Weren't you already doing that with us?" Dara asked. "Not that there's anything wrong with that. Collegial consultation; all in a day's work. Anyway you didn't give our names to the *Times*."

"I wouldn't have done that without asking. But thanks. So what if I do ask now? They're not going to want me hemming and hawing on my own."

"Well," Malcolm grinned, "we can do that with you. Sometimes it's the best thing. Put a question mark after an attribution and see what happens. Besides, we've only seen photographs. But what about the Venice picture?"

"Who's actually seen it, you mean. Terterian's student Regina has, so far as I know. But my friend Letizia Bassani at the Accademia is on the case. She's not saying much, though; beyond trying to figure out whether it's in Venice because it never left or whether it came back somehow. How that rich Italian, Brambilla, got it. She says it's a pretty slow chase, whatever that means."

8

There was no use resisting Flavia's offer to stay with her after the break-in. It was more like an order and Regina didn't have any better ideas. She quickly stuffed some essentials into a suitcase and a shopping bag and followed Flavia in a daze to the vaporetto stop. She felt as if she had been run over by the dark alter ego of carnival revelry. She could use a break at Flavia's place.

"I promised to be on the job for the English couple later this morning," Flavia said when she let Regina into her top floor apartment in backwater Santa Croce. "I'm already late. Settle in and we'll try to figure out what's going on when I get back."

"You're a lifesaver, *cara*. Thank you." Regina didn't say more, but she was glad not to be making decisions. She would sit back first and collect her thoughts later. It would be an innocent distraction and she could make up for lost time—that's what she was feeling about Giovanni now—and see what she had missed. Logging in to her email account on Flavia's computer, she found, mixed with the inevitable spam, a message from Terterian wondering whether she had any new leads, notes from friends imagining her prancing around in some lavish carnival costume, and a tease from her brother about his *dolce vita* sister. She almost deleted a message from an Italian address she didn't recognize after reading the first lines in strained English.

> *Gentile dottoressa, I have not had the pleasure of your acquaintance and hesitate to write to you without a proper introduction. I pray that you will excuse this intrusion for the sake of a matter that is, I believe, of concern to the both of us.*

Probably a scam, a nosey reporter at the *Gazzettino*, whatever. She read on anyway; it might be a comfort to have company for "a concern to both of us," whatever that might be.

> *I have read of your interest in images of San Maurizio, painted, it is said, by Giotto. I have reason to believe that an early example of the saint's image passed through Siena before being dispersed. I shall not go into details here.*

The matter would best be treated in person and perhaps you will be so kind as to accept my invitation to meet in Siena at your convenience.

With distinct regards,
Giovanna Giovannoni

Siena? Siena hadn't come up in her research. Someone could be putting her on. Drawn by news stories and trolling for some payoff. It might be dangerous—a baited hook. Art world egos and big money were on the line. The rough stuff at the Campo San Maurizio and the break-in had left her feeling vulnerable.

Regina was fuming by the time that Flavia returned. She handed her the letter she had printed out. "Look at this. My convenience! I'm supposed to traipse off to Siena, just like that."

Flavia read the letter while Regina paced. "*Calma, cara!* Don't be silly. You need to get away. You won't miss our narcissism down there. Siena's got more of that for its size than we do. And who knows what this lady's got?"

***

Regina felt a surge of relief after crossing the lagoon to the mainland. The *Freccia d'Argento*, the "Silver Arrow," flew through the little universes of towns snubbed by high speed rails. Names for fast trains were a classic study in Italian marketing genius. The old *Rapido*, always an optimistic name for those brown caterpillar-looking postwar conveyances, had been demoted. Most of the time but not always, the bullet-nosed *Freccia* with its "High Velocity" billing did the 150 miles to Florence in two hours before the old order took its revenge. The local trains from Florence to Siena could take almost that long for 45 miles—longer, as Regina had the misfortune to find out, if you missed the right connection.

Arriving, finally, at a Fascist-era station that looked more anachronistic than the 17th-century Camollia gate just beyond it, she had another mile and a half to go on a bus that wound around the walls and parking lots with only teasing glimpses of the famous sights that always looked close in pictures. At the stop the driver indicated, she still had an uphill walk to the center of town.

Giovanna Giovannoni had suggested meeting for an *aperitivo* at one of the outdoor cafes in the scallop shell shaped piazza anchoring the civic center in the Campo, the low lying "field" between Siena's three hills. The medieval city fathers had decreed that the campanile of the city hall had to be the tallest building in town, topping the battlements of a trouble-making nobility and the spires of the bishop's cathedral. Like many things in Siena, the rules hadn't changed all that much.

Regina knew from earlier visits that it wasn't easy to get to the Campo. Siena, like Venice, was a maze and mostly car-free, but without canals or a good supply of water. With the campanile as her compass, she finally came to a relatively wide, fairly straight street of gray paving stones where late afternoon strollers were out to socialize and show themselves off. The direction seemed right, but at a bend between close files of brick and stone facades she lost sight of the campanile; not for the first time. Turning to backtrack, she glanced down a narrow passageway on her left and saw a slice of the Campo that, with a few more steps, suddenly opened in a flash of curves and colors.

Regina almost forgot why she was there. You were never really prepared for the Photoshop-free "burnt Siena" colors ribbed with whitish stone, the three dimensions, the movement, the soft echo of conversation. The campanile on the flank of the city hall, the Palazzo Pubblico, looked like it might take off like a rocket. The café umbrellas around the perimeter of the Campo fluttered in tribute like a *corps de ballet.*

It was an effort to turn away from the view to the messages from Siena. Cryptic, with a dubious claim about a San Maurizio picture and an invitation to come for an *aperitivo* on the Campo. There must be dozens of Giovannas and probably more than a few Giovannonis in Siena. Regina checked her purse for the invitation again: a woman wearing the green scarf with red and white stripes of the Contrada dell'Oca, one of those famously tight-knit Sienese neighborhood societies, would expect her at the Bar al Palio on the Campo at 18:00.

That was identification enough as it turned out. She saw the name on a choreographical formation of umbrellas. A green, red, and white scarf stood out in the mix of tourists and the locals priming for the ritual evening walk. The wearer showed no apparent surprise at the approach of a young black woman. The surprise was Regina's. She wondered a little uneasily how much this person would have found out about her. From the tone of the email she had expected an older woman. But old-fashioned Italian courtesy across generations was part of keeping up appearances. This woman looked like she might be in her forties—women's ages were usually a guess in Italy. She rose, extended her hand, and invited Regina to join her at a table with view facing the Campo. Lights would soon be illuminating the Palazzo Pubblico, still the seat of the city government, and the architectural variations modeled on its façade around the piazza.

"Welcome to Siena, dottoressa. It is very kind of you to respond to our invitation."

Regina settled into the chair offered to her and returned the proper courtesies—her gratitude for the invitation; the beauty of the city; the marvel of the Campo—while waiting for some explanation. "My aunt Giovanna—I am her niece, Caterina—apologizes for not being able to welcome you in person. She is obliged to keep indoors much of the time now, but she wanted me to meet you here. She was concerned that you might have some difficulty finding the way to her. She also said that I could show off the Campo this way without seeming to boast. What may I offer you?"

"I'll have whatever you're having." Regina nodded towards what looked like a glass of Cinzano with ice and a slice of lemon. "Venice is good practice for finding your way," she added.

"From what we know, you seem to have found your way quite well in Venice. Finding things nobody knew much of anything about."

"I've been lucky, I guess." Regina held back troubling things that she knew too little about.

***

Regina's meeting in the Campo left her guessing. But the window of her little tower room in the Albergo Antica Torre made up for that. The view was a perfect miniature of the campanile rising over the black-and-white striped cathedral on the facing hill. Distraction was a Sienese specialty after the Black Death made time slow down, stop, or run backwards to spite the present.

With her eye still on the view, Regina reached for the map Giovannoni's niece had drawn on a napkin when inviting her for tea at her Aunt Giovanna's apartment. "She is eager to meet you, but she says that we must be patient and give you time to explore. She is sure that you will want to see our paintings; we like to believe they outshine those of the early Florentines, even Giotto's."

Regina realized that she would need plenty of time for the route that looked easy on paper. Siena was GPS-resistant. There were high and low curves on the ground and unnamed forks where Caterina Giovannoni had shown straight lines. Her destination was Vicolo de' Pittori, 16, which translated as "Painters' Alley," correctly enough about its being like an alleyway as it turned out. According to the makeshift map, she was supposed to follow the Via de' Pittori, then in one or maybe two turns come to a narrow branch off from it. The first corner, with no street sign, looked unpromising; there was no sign at the second corner, either, but Regina could see a lineup of protruding doorbell pulls, the old-fashioned brass knobs that had mostly stopped working many years earlier.

Taking her chances, she turned into the tight street, stopping as she walked to read numbers and names below the brass knobs. Next to an arch leading into a courtyard she found a small plaque inscribed with the address she was looking for. Relieved, she pulled the knob under the name "Giovanna Chiarini nei Giovannoni" and waited. She was about to try again when the door opened at the top of the stairs on one side of the courtyard. Caterina Giovannoni emerged and waved her up.

She greeted Regina like a friend, with open arms. Had Regina passed a test of some sort without knowing it? It was probably just that warm welcomes prevailed in Italy once you crossed the family threshold. Regina expressed thanks for the invitation. She didn't mention the map.

"My aunt is so pleased," Caterina repeated as she led Regina from the circle of the entry hall into a spacious room with pale walls and a rustic, dark-beamed ceiling. The room looked as if it had been sealed sometime around 1500, then opened again in the 1920s or 30s. The furnishings were spare, but each of the older pieces was a minor monument in its own right: a Renaissance trestle table in dark wood; a painted wedding chest; four high-backed chairs with leather seats and leather backs held by brass studs. Two Sienese Madonnas hung on facing walls in gilded frames. Padded armchairs and a sofa had been tastefully added, for comfort, judging from their worn striped fabric.

"I hope you will excuse me, dottoressa, for not coming to meet you earlier," the old lady on the sofa said in the soft accents that didn't travel well beyond Tuscany. "You see I am bound to this house and to that contraption now." Regina would not have guessed as much if her hostess had not pointed to a wheelchair in the corner. She was small, even tiny, but not at all frail looking, with her sharp profile, long mauve dress, and elegant silvery shawl of finely woven wool. She gestured toward the silver tea service and a plate of cookies dusted with powdered sugar on the chest that served as a table. "Perhaps you will allow me to make small amends by offering you tea and our Sienese *ricciolini.* Please sit here beside me and let Caterina pour tea for us."

Regina made the only possible response, accepting the offer and easing herself onto the sofa while Caterina poured tea into china cups with gold rims and a Sienese black-and-white design. The old lady gestured with a proprietary sweep of her hand, "I grew up in this house, you know. My father moved us here. That was before the war." She pointed to a photograph in a silver frame. "My father in his studio."

The confident-looking man with a well-trimmed gray moustache was wearing an old-fashioned smock and a beret. He wielded a long-handled brush in his right hand as if sizing up the next stroke. Regina waited for her hostess to continue.

"Some of my first memories are of that studio and its 'perfume,' as my father liked to say. I loved to watch him mix pigments. He would have none of the new ones in his studio, just the old vermilion, verdigris, yellow oxide, even expensive lapis lazuli blue that came from Afghanistan. I imagined him as one of the old masters he took me to see in the galleries at the Pinacoteca. He liked to talk about how they worked. It was not just talk of course."

She reached for a scrapbook-sized album beside her on a pillow. "This is the only one left now." She looked away before handing it to Regina. "The others were lost during the war. Terrible to think of."

Regina handled the album carefully. It looked like it might contain about thirty bound pages and some loose sheets. "You may open it," Giovannoni said.

It was evidently a sketchbook and portfolio. Turning the first few pages, Regina found sketches and more or less finished drawings on some bound pages, with sheets of varying sizes attached or loosely inserted between them. "You see, our great painters were his first love." The old lady watched closely. Regina recognized details drawn from the trinity of early Sienese painters: Duccio, Simone Martini, Ambrogio Lorenzetti.

"But he wanted to learn from the old masters wherever he could. The other painters in town then—there were lots of old style painters here in those days—made fun of him about that. 'So we're not good enough for you, Duccio. You're named after our great painter and you go around copying the Florentines. It's a disgrace!'"

Giovannoni chuckled as she beckoned Regina to turn the pages. "You see. Giotto. The Arena Chapel." And indeed, there were the heads of Joachim and Anna, tipping tenderly toward one another, and several sketches of their draperies; on the next page studies of standing figures from the Arena. Looking ever more intently, Regina came to studies of Arena figures drawn in different postures. Drawings from the Flagellation scene were among them. She stared as if needing to convince herself about what she was seeing, until, finally, she turned the page. And there, on the next sheet, were Chiarini's variations on the Arena's black man, his stick upraised, the head in profile, then reimagined in three quarter profiles and full face, then again standing as in the fresco, but also drawn from different viewpoints.

"My father was a *maestro*, you see." Regina did see. She was transfixed. That was evidently answer enough. Her hostess sat quietly watching until the sound of footsteps finally broke the spell.

"That will be my niece. I asked her to leave us alone for a while, but she will be coming to check on the old lady. Perhaps she will let us meet again tomorrow. You can look again. There's more to see, but never enough, never enough, I'm afraid."

"Ah, Caterina, so soon. But it doesn't matter. I have invited the dottoressa to join me again tomorrow, unless she finds other diversions." The old lady took the next visit as a foregone conclusion. "So, we are agreed." Regina, stunned, almost curtseyed before Caterina led her to the top of the stairs.

"My aunt is difficult, I'm afraid. She tires easily and that annoys her. She forgets things. Not the old days, though. She worshipped her father. Seeing the news about San Maurizio in the papers she remembered his sketches. She'll probably want to tell you more tomorrow."

***

I'd better recover from today first, Regina thought as she went down the stairs into the courtyard and through the arch into the narrow passageway. As if by the force of gravity, she was drawn into the late afternoon procession toward the Campo. The dawdling pace was slow, so she took a sharp turn away from the crowd up toward the cathedral, thinking that its stripes of black and white stone would be soothing and help her focus.

She stopped for a breather before climbing the steep steps alongside the baptistry at the choir end of the church. There was a large rectangle of open space at the top of the stairs in the skeleton of the massive extension of the cathedral that the Sienese began to build in the 14th century. The Black Death put an end to that fit of grandiosity in 1348. Regina walked toward the end of what would have been the new nave and sat down on a ledge where she could survey the measured order of the striped cathedral wall without the visual commotion of pink moldings and holy messengers on the façade.

Was the background of the stripes black or white? She hadn't thought of them that way before, but she liked the idea of getting some sympathetic feedback. On whether San Maurizio was black or white, or somehow both.

She decided to start counting from the ground up, trying to sort out what she had heard and seen. A *maestro,* Giovannoni had called her father. The Italians bestowed that title on any skilled professional, and some unskilled ones; it was what a dutiful daughter would say. But Regina had to agree, judging from the album. About what, though? This Duccio was a skilled copyist. Yes, certainly, but more than that in his variations taking off from the originals. They were inventions, yet they looked plausible, like variations—did she really believe this?—that Giotto himself might have made.

But why? Giovannoni said her father was always learning. Regina was sure that she meant more than studying in the abstract, something more like continuing, even reliving the old ways of working.

That wasn't supposed to be possible. Art historians made a profession out of telling you it wasn't. To every work of art its own time and place and all that. "We"—Regina parroted the pontificating pronoun—"can assure you that forgers, especially forgers of old paintings, give themselves away in telltale anachronisms and infelicities that our expertise will expose to vindicate true and authentic mastery in art."

This brought to mind a quotable she had read somewhere: "The past is a foreign country; they do things differently there." Giovannoni might say instead that her father believed—sincerely—that the past could be a familiar country; and that was why he was the *maestro* he was. Regina was not immune to such professional heresies. "Sincere" didn't have to mean truly singular, individual, or original. It could just as well suggest absorption in a shared past. She was seeing something like that all around her Siena.

But she wasn't quite sure how the *maestro*'s studies of the black flagellant could be sincere if he made them to paint a San Maurizio that could pass for Giotto's work. Maybe he had more than the Arena image or his imagination to go on. Say, a picture to restore so as—Regina could imagine him thinking this—to bring it back to life. There was a tenuous line between restoring and faking. Siena had been famous for both, notorious too.

The black on white or white on black stripes had helped her to sort some things out. Not everything, though. The black San Maurizio could be a restoration or a forgery. What did that mean for Brambilla's white San Maurizio? Was one or the other the real thing in her archival find?

***

On the way back to the Vicolo de' Pittori, more directly this time, Regina made a mental note of a title she saw in a bookstore window—*Siena: City of Secrets*. She supposed you could say that about any city, especially in Italy with so many centuries available for historical hide-and-seek. Then again, all that accumulated experience in close quarters meant that there wasn't much room for hiding secrets; they were bound to come out sooner or later for everyone who cared, outsiders excepted.

So why did Giovanna Giovannoni reveal so much to me? Regina wondered. Or maybe it wasn't a revelation. The family probably knew most of it; maybe the whole neighborhood did. But they apparently hadn't known before about the two San Maurizio paintings. The niece told her that her aunt was obsessed by the news; it had prompted old memories that led her to reach out to Regina.

Caterina came out from the courtyard before Regina could pull the doorbell knob. "My aunt asked me to look out for you. She's anxious to get on with your conversation."

"But I hardly said a word. There was so much to take in."

"Well, it was a big day for her. She went through the album again this morning. She hadn't looked at it for a long time; she keeps turning the pages now. We already knew a lot about my uncle's work."

Caterina turned back as she led Regina up the stairs. "Just restoration work of course. You can see some of the pictures he restored at the Pinacoteca."

The old lady was on her feet this time. "Your visit yesterday gave me much pleasure, dottoressa." She invited Regina to resume her former place on the sofa as she settled into her own. The album lay open on the chest between them. "But there is more, you know. I would like to show you something else and then we shall have our tea."

"Something else that survived the war?" Regina asked.

"Survived the war. Yes. And my father's death. Before it was over."

The loss, after all that time, brought tears to the old lady's eyes. She recovered quickly, but Regina reminded herself that the pull of the past was not just about material things or her own obsessions. She resolved not to need reminding again.

"It's something in the album."

"The same one, Signora?"

"There are no others." Giovannoni reached out, touched the album reverently, then opened it carefully to the studies of the Arena flagellation. The drawing looked as brilliant as it had the day before.

"I believe you will remember that we stopped here yesterday, dottoressa. I wanted to give you a proper finale and did not wish to disappoint you. The next page, this one, is not beautiful, but you may find it interesting enough to make up for that."

Regina saw what looked a heading or an address near the top of a sheet of scrap paper. A line of few words had been scratched out below, evidently by the same hand.

"My father's writing. An address on this side for a letter, with a date: *Zorzi/ Pal.zo Villa Maravegie, 1935*. I thought you might be able to help me with them."

"Because the names look Venetian." Regina thought for a moment. "Zorzi certainly. The family had a medieval doge, I think, but it's a common name. And there's a Maravegie bridge. In Dorsoduro, across Rio San Trovaso. Maybe he means a palazzo near there. It wouldn't be far from the dealers' galleries around the Accademia."

"Thank you, dottoressa. The address of a correspondent in Venice, a dealer perhaps. That seems likely enough from what I can read on the other side. I have studied it closely. Not so legible, I'm afraid; would you be so kind…? "

Regina scanned the page turned toward her. There were three fragments, evidently in Duccio Chiarini's hand, not so much paragraphs as notes or memoranda, almost in code, with lines drawn between them. Taking the magnifying glass on the chest, she read painstakingly, first to herself, then aloud.

Object entrusted to my care safe, out of sight—our hills Himalayas of rumor/ gossip/ envy. Protest against too much haste, little understanding.

~

Full attention given since yours of xxxx; neither too much ardor nor too much restraint. Where add, where withhold? Question in life as in art. You/ client to be satisfied...

~

"Deplorable tradition?" Swear by S. Maurizio and my old Latin teacher Tozzi's lessons that I shall "find" for your learned Germans the panel suited to them.

When Regina had finished reading, as best she could, aloud, Giovannoni asked—it was not so much a question as a confirmation—"That's all then."

"I can't make out anything else, Signora."

"So tell me what you make of the texts you can read. Notes we might call them."

"Yes. I'd say for letters to a Zorzi; in Venice, in 1935. It looks like this Zorzi was some kind of dealer and in that case the 'object' entrusted to your father could be the panel in the last note. For restoration."

She stopped. "But 'learned Germans' and 'S. Maurizio...' The old German emperors had a cult of San Maurizio and Nazi propaganda took it over in the 1930s."

The old lady, who had been signaling her agreement all along, drew herself up straight, bristling. "You must not believe, dottoressa, that my father would have had anything to do with that. He hated the Fascists; when the Germans occupied us in '43, he helped the partisans fighting them both. That's why his studio was sacked. He escaped just in time. Took what he could south toward Marchese Origo's big estate in the Val d'Orcia. The Marchese and his English wife sheltered everyone they could. People bombed out, soldiers trying to get home, prisoners escaping." Giovannoni's vehemence trailed off to a murmur. "My father was trying to reach the allied lines, but they were stalled in the south. We never saw him again."

The tea Caterina Giovannoni had laid out had turned cold and was forgotten.

***

Regina's carriage in the balky local train back to Florence was nearly empty. She imagined it as a stage and began assigning seats to characters in her little drama. It didn't bother her that the cast was not complete and the order of appearances was not set. She knew that Enrico Scrovegni and Giotto belonged up front. Without them she wouldn't be sitting where she was at all. She knew them better than some people she could see and touch in the flesh. She certainly knew them better than the saint who was a focus of so much attention while remaining frustratingly elusive. Maurizio, protagonist though he was, would have to go somewhere in the back, maybe in more than one seat since he had been recast for so many purposes. That had happened again in Siena.

She hadn't known about Duccio Chiarini. She still didn't know much of anything for certain about the "Zorzi" in Chiarini's notes. But Chiarini deserved a place near Giotto; exactly where, remained to be seen. Maybe Brambilla belonged near Scrovegni as the latest patron of Giotto and of San Maurizio. He would like that; even, she supposed, insist on it. Other characters might be waiting in the wings, not just Zorzi. Sooner or later she would have to find room somewhere for Terterian and Farber—and herself for that matter.

She had put off reporting to Terterian again since the break-in. She didn't want him to think she was asking for sympathy and she hadn't known what to expect in Siena. She didn't feel comfortable with another round of placeholding phrases: "a few setbacks but a few new leads... promising... not sure yet... more soon." But she was reluctant to risk more too soon or get sucked into Phyllis Farber's schemes.

When they had talked on the phone after New York but before the break-in, Terterian sounded too close to Farber for comfort. Regina's anyway. "She's heading for the big auction in London," he had said, as if it were his business to keep up with Farber. "She's going to look at the supposed Caravaggio that turned up in some gloomy parish in Ireland; check out what they're saying is a Duccio Madonna coming out of a Swiss bank vault." Regina didn't care about Farber's calendar until he coyly, too coyly, remarked: "I'm sure you can guess what else is on her schedule."

Yes, she could, but she was not in the mood for guessing games and waited for him to answer for himself that Farber had big plans for her San Maurizio, "even bigger than you might think." A blockbuster show at the Met for her San Maurizio and Cranach's German black St. Moritz that had been given to the museum out of the blue. There's talk of trying to bring over the medieval sculptures from Magdeburg or even Grünewald's marvelous picture of Moritz meeting St. Erasmus from Munich. It would ordinarily take years to arrange anything like that, but Phyllis was shopping headlines to get on the fast track: "Two Masterpieces of a Black Saint

Rediscovered; Diversity and Tolerance in the Canon of Western Art; Multicultural Coup at the Met."

Regina had asked as steadily as she could manage whether Farber was saying that the New York picture was authentic and that she could prove it. In her heart of hearts she would actually like to believe that Giotto had painted a black San Maurizio. All the more so if he had done it for one of the premier patrons of early Renaissance art. This would confirm the narrative about Giotto's inventiveness; it could update the old story as an artifact of the worldly openness of the Renaissance without the snarky condescension or the politically correct harangues against European imperialism that were all the rage. Besides, it would be a comfort to have Giotto and San Maurizio on her side as a black Renaissance art historian. She was even tempted to agree that Phyllis Farber's headlines got it right.

"Authentic?" Terterian had said. "Phyllis hasn't claimed that in so many words. But the Met's not going to reject a plausible Giotto out of hand, and Phyllis can round up enough Giotto scholars to tell her what she wants to hear.

"If there are doubts?"

Terterian took a bow to relative truths. "Well, no one is going to be totally certain. If you don't have negative proof."

"But Farber will have to say where picture came from. How she got it. She hasn't done that yet."

"She says she's got a good family story. Just needs to doctor it a little. There's a grand tradition for that."

Regina had pictured Terterian's smirk. "She'll say it was a gift from an Italian family to the American soldier who rescued one of them from the Germans or maybe from the Fascists during World War II. It had been taken down at some point and stored away, then forgotten until the old family house had to be cleared out. No one paid much attention; the picture was not in good shape. But someone thought it ought to be appraised. That's how it got to Phyllis. She had it cleaned up enough to recognize what it really was. That's probably enough to get by."

"And we're—I'm—supposed to go along with that."

"Less convincing stories make the cut all the time. This one is probably close enough to what happened."

"Even if we need to know more."

"Even if it's probably going to a winner for the Met? And for you? Don't ask so many questions, Regina. You shouldn't worry so much."

Regina hadn't answered. But that was before the break-in. And before Siena. She braced herself for telling Terterian that she would not be going along, at least on Farber's terms. The New York picture must be Chiarini's work; it had probably got to the U.S. as an American G.I.'s booty.

9

Flavia texted that she would be waiting at the San Marcuola vaporetto stop, the second stop from Santa Lucia station. It took its name from one of those Venetian churches named in opportunistic pairings of Greek and Latin saints so as to corner the market in blessings from the East and West. The stop named after the church was the stop for the Casino, a latterday version of Venice combining profit and piety. Regina had no interest in gambling, not for money anyway. Besides, she was put off by the plaque about the death of Richard Wagner in the Renaissance palace that had become a classy gambling hall. Her taste hadn't progressed, if she could put it that way, much beyond early Verdi. But why did Flavia want to meet at the San Marcuola stop?

Regina edged off the boat through a crowd of irritable Venetians and oblivious tourists just as Flavia was just rounding the corner at San Marcuola. She picked up Regina's bag with a hug and a business-like greeting. "It's this way."

"*Scusa, cara.* What is this way?"

"Your new place," Flavia interrupted. "You can't go back to the old one, so we moved you."

"You what!"

"You left me the key. The old landlady was cooperative; she had you pegged as trouble. You won't miss the old dump. My cousin knew about this apartment."

Regina had actually been thinking about moving. Maybe to somewhere in Castello where there were more real Venetians and the rents were more affordable.

"It's next to the Grand Canal, but don't worry about the rent. It's on the ground floor in the backside of a palazzo; so you get low rent and maybe a touch of *acqua alta* instead of a view. Come on, you'll like it well enough."

Between resignation and relief, Regina followed Flavia towards the Strada Nova, then into a narrow passageway after crossing a small bridge named *Ponte Storto* after its odd angle. Another still smaller bridge made out of wood led through a *sottoportego* under an overhang into a large courtyard, the *Cortile Michiel della Commedia.*

"That's it," said Flavia, pointing to a green door straight ahead and handing Regina a set of keys. "So let me in. We'll make coffee and you can tell me what you found out in Siena."

The apartment was narrow. It had probably been storage room for the galley trade, a rundown worker's hovel, most recently a conversion for the Airbnb market. The furnishings must have come from IKEA. Regina liked the hygienic Swedish look contrasting with rough wooden beams and the terrazzo floor. Everything essential was there, including her clothes in a pine chest, a white desk on wrought iron legs, and an espresso machine. Flavia was right that she wouldn't be missing the old place.

Regina charged the coffee machine with the Illy grind she found in a cupboard and made a double espresso for them both. "I can't thank you enough, you know," she said as they sat down in the niche of a room next to the kitchen."

"Well, it's clean, as our mothers would say. But never mind the thanks and just tell me about Siena."

Too many details would have sounded even more unbelievable than they were in fact. Flavia was quick with the right questions about the abbreviated version and some that Regina would rather not have heard.

"So it's pretty clear that this Sienese guy, Chiarini, must have worked on a San Maurizio picture, a black one. Was it a restoration job or did he make it up from the black Arena figure? And Brambilla. He's made a big deal about his picture. Maybe he set you up with Giovanni Bonelli. Anyway, it's not likely you'll be seeing more of Giovanni, is it?"

"No, it isn't," Regina responded to the one question she had a clear answer for.

"But you can't just ignore Brambilla. And he needs to talk to you."

"I don't know that 'needs' is the right word."

Flavia rubbed her thumb and fingers together. "You should cash in on him while you can; come out with the Siena story to make his picture look like the real thing. He'll make it worth your while."

Regina ignored the invitation to blackmail. "Not when I'm not sure, about him or his picture."

"So you'll just wait for someone else to give him what he wants? The big shots are not going to trip him up. They're the ones who need to worry. Indictments coming down on the Consorzio gang. And now Letizia Bassani's involved. You remember her?"

"Sure. She worked with you at San Giacomo; got lucky with the Accademia job. But what does she…"

Flavia cut in with an Italian *si dice*, "it's said," that makes gossip sound objective without taking personal responsibility for it. "*Si dice* that she's assigned to the Brambilla Case. You two should get together."

Like any good Venetian following the story, Letizia Bassani took it for granted that Regina Payne would side with her American countrymen—birds of a feather and all that. And with the New York picture on account of her color too. After meeting with the Director of the Accademia Letizia secretly hoped that was the case. Her task would be easier if the New York picture trumped Brambilla's version. That would make his picture all the more suspect.

There was nothing to lose by talking to Regina. Jeremy Hammond had dared her; that usually meant that he was serious and, usually too, that he was right. "She may be playing hard to get," he said. "People at the Met would like to see what she's got for a big black saints show here. I'd say you've got more than enough white saints over there already, but we could always use some black ones. You know, for diversity."

With what she regarded as a pardonable touch of cunning, Letizia mailed Regina inviting her to join her for tea or a drink: they had friends and interests in common; they should get to know one another better; etc. Letizia hinted that they probably would agree about a particular interest they shared at the moment. She didn't mention the litany of allegations against Brambilla. The records for missing or stolen art were incomplete, often deliberately so, but like trying on shoes for size, Letizia was looking for a fit for at least one of the charges.

There was still a twilight glow as Regina crossed the Accademia bridge into Dorsoduro. Just the right atmosphere for confidences. She was not certain she wanted to oblige. Meeting over a glass of wine at Il Bottegon was not her idea.

Letizia was talking animatedly with a couple in the overflow crowd when she arrived at the old wine bar. Catching sight of Regina, she waved her over and introduced her friends Sergio and Marina, adding as if there were any doubt, "We've known one another forever, since school days; they can spare me this one time."

She pulled Regina away for the conversation they were both uneasy about. "Let me bring you something from the counter," she said. "I'm a regular so we won't have to wait. My apologies for not asking you sooner. My new job is taking up a lot of time, but that's not a good excuse."

"No need for to apologize. A prosecco would be fine. I've been away, and I had some trouble in my old apartment and had to leave it in a rush and move into a new place."

Letizia shook her head sympathetically as she went for their drinks.

"Things are better now?" she said on returning with two glasses to their perch on the wall next to the Rio San Trovaso.

"Yes, better."

"Let's drink to that," said Letizia, raising her glass. "It might help if I say that most Venetians are going to agree with you about the San Maurizio pictures. It's not my field, but you can't be an art historian in this town without having an opinion." She came to the point. "That is, if you think there's a good case for the one in New York. The one here—well, there are all sorts of problems about it."

Regina's put her glass down slowly. Letizia took this as a signal to lay out the charges against Brambilla. Before she had finished, she was painfully aware that she still had little if any hard evidence to back them up. Either from the art history literature or the databases on missing or stolen art. "The thing is," she hesitated, "I'm under a lot of pressure to tell the higher-ups what they want to hear."

"I can understand that," Regina said quietly.

To Letizia's disappointment, the conversation turned after that in different directions. She didn't succeed in getting it back on track, but as they got up to leave, she suggested that it would be a good idea for them to keep in touch.

Regina's "it might be" was non-committal. For good reasons. Letizia had all but admitted to being on assignment to dig up dirt on Brambilla. Giotto and San Maurizio were probably not what she—or her superiors—were really after. In any case it wasn't at all clear what to say about the New York picture. Doing nothing wasn't an acceptable option after Siena. She would feel—she would be—guilty of betraying Giovanna Giovannoni's trust, her own conscience, and, pretentious as it sounded, her sense of professional responsibility. The thought that it mattered to Giotto was even fuzzier, but she was not going to betray him either.

And Terterian. Maybe she should have been upfront with him. Her reluctance had turned into unwillingness to cooperate with Farber or, if it came to that, with him. She wanted to believe that he would back her up, but he had sounded like he might brush her off. The Chiarini connection was bound to come to light sooner or later.

Why not sooner? Let Giotto scholars, Terterian, and Phyllis Farber make of it what they would.

***

"What are you saying, John?" Phyllis Farber's voice cracked. She looked around to see if anyone in the Madison Room bar was listening. "You can't be serious."

John Terterian had decided he needed to let Farber know in person what Regina had called to tell him the day before. He was giving another lecture in New York and arranged to meet her afterwards. He said he had news from Venice she needed to hear before putting finishing touches on her big San Maurizio plans. And, keeping this to himself, before he could decide how far he was going to cooperate with her.

"I am serious, Phyllis."

"Trusting this black girl, your art historian in training. With that ridiculous name." She scoffed, again too loudly. "Regina, wanting her little moment of glory. Come on, John, she's in over her head."

"Maybe. But she's not the only one."

"Meaning?" Farber was not taking hints.

"Well, she asked if she could take a few photos. The Chiarini woman didn't want her to."

"How convenient for her, John." Farber leaned back and signaled for another drink. "The Met people will be amused, I'm sure. Those drawings must be hack work tricked out in an old lady's gossip."

Terterian shrugged off the tirade, "Regina persuaded her that it was time to celebrate her father's mastery and his story, something like that. Anyway, the old lady finally agreed and let her photograph some of his studies made from Giotto's black flagellant in the Scrovegni chapel."

"Which you've seen?"

Reaching down, Terterian pulled a manila folder out of his computer case. "I printed these out from Regina's attachment."

Farber left the folder unopened on the table between them. "And this proves—what?" she said with a contemptuous gesture as if to banish the offending object. "That this man knew how to use pencil and chalk, that he did some drawings from Giotto. It's been happening for ages."

"Why don't you just have a look."

"So I can say that he could have done whatever is in your folder from my original." She waited.

"I suppose you could say that."

"You know, John," Farber said with an icy stare, "what I will say again is that you had better watch out for your Regina. Doors closing on her career before it gets started. Her adviser wouldn't want that. He would ask her to be more professional, more cooperative."

"So we'll both be on board."

Farber's stare devolved into a tight smile. "That's part of it."

"And casting her off if you need to?"

"I suppose that remains to be seen."

***

The fog was still billowing over the Palazzo Bastagli when Piergiorgio Brambilla finished his morning coffee. It would soon give way to bursts of sunlight. He was an appreciative observer of the atmospheric shifts in Venice that were predictable without ever being quite the same.

Conversations with his friend Paolo Michiel in the Procurator's office were like that. You could never be altogether certain whether Michiel was acting officially or as a solicitous friend, whether he was fishing for inside information or revealing it. This time Brambilla expected some of both.

Michiel had slipped through the private entrance of the palazzo. He wanted to avoid the eavesdropping in the usual watering holes where Gasparo Corner and the gossip hunters would be on the prowl. He thought Brambilla should know, he wanted to say, if he didn't know already, that the Soprintendenza and the Accademia had joined the Consorzio campaign against him. The Director at the Accademia had put a certain Letizia Bassani on the case. Young, new over there, easier to manage than the old hands; from a good enough but not overbearing Venetian family. That's why she got the job of course. Bassani would know her way around without attracting attention if she were curious about who's doing what.

"I have to admit, Piergiorgio, that the clueless outsider, pompous *foresto* of a Director though he is, was right to put Bassani on the case, even if he didn't understand it was not going to stay secret for long. Everybody knows by now that she's cozied up to that black girl you showed your Giotto to."

"Things everybody knows aren't of much interest; much less interesting than things we don't know about. Surely you agree, Paolo.

"Why my office has been instructed to undertake investigations on our own, for example?"

"Yes, that could be interesting." Brambilla had inferred from the start that this was what Michiel had come to tell him.

Michiel left the inference hanging until he was ready. "Or just routine. Tiresome. Boring. To be on the look-out all the time. Like Argos with all those eyes."

"With certain rewards too, you must admit. Such as knowing all about what your dear colleagues policing the world are up to."

"Blind justice—an absurd idea, don't you agree, Piergiorgio? Dangerous too."

Brambilla stuck to his point. "So by the same token they must know what you're doing."

"Not exactly." Michiel glided toward disclosure. "They seem to think they can show that your picture was stolen. Not much to that. You wouldn't have called attention to it if they could prove that."

"It might be risky."

Realizing that Brambilla was not going to give away who or what might be at risk, Michiel forged ahead. "Interpol, Carabinieri, NGOs are busy enough just listing missing and stolen art, let alone finding it. Antiquities dug up, a big money crop in the south. Museum heists everywhere, like the big one in Verona; little ones like that beautiful little Bellini over in the Madonna dell'Orto. Claims still coming in about pictures the Nazis forced

110

people to sell cheap, or just robbed outright before sending them to the camps. Anyway, we know they're not going to identify your San Maurizio in those lists, don't we?"

Brambilla shifted in his chair and left that question unanswered too.

"You know I would have steered clear of this business if I could have. My office is good at looking the other way. The trouble is it's *acqua alta* season for scandal right now. Damned if we don't investigate, damned when we do. You understand that we need to look like we're hot on the trail of something or other."

Michiel took a deep breath to emphasize how much farther he was going to go. "That black American girl, chasing after Giotto and San Maurizio and taking liberties with you. You'll understand why we needed, shall I say, to search her apartment to find out what she knows. It looks like she's covered her tracks; or maybe we don't know what to look for. Probably some of both?" The question fell flat, as Michiel must have known it would. He had made it clear enough that the "search" had not produced evidence against Brambilla.

But he was not quite finished yet. "About the war. The old picture dealers were thrilled when 'the ridiculous little Austrian painter' came to meet Il Duce here in 1934. They must have cheered with the huge crowd in San Marco. They were already cashing in on their new wave of German customers from Nazi bigwigs on down. Your San Maurizio would have been a prize if anyone knew about it."

"I suppose so," Brambilla said. "Too bad Hitler didn't stick to his brushes."

***

The protocol was the same as before: the servant at the entrance; the grand staircase up to the long hall. Regina had expected an invitation to the Palazzo Bastagli for another "informal conversation." Brambilla's timing was unnerving all the same. He seemed to anticipate when something important turned up. Flavia's line about his "making it worth your while" to know what she had found out in Siena might not be so far fetched. She would let him take the lead. Not that she could do otherwise.

As before, Brambilla was in no hurry as he led her from the processional route to his comfortable retreat. He offered her coffee and invited her to choose from the delicacies on the antique silver tray. He called her attention to the view. "Interesting that the best representations of the changing atmosphere in Venice are by your Americans. Whistler and Sargent. But you Americans are not burdened by fixed habits and can see things afresh and then move on when you like."

Whistler and Sargent were not exactly her Americans, but Venetian atmospherics were obviously not his point, either. Behind his Old World indirection they both understood he was angling for an update from her and maybe more besides.

He shifted, this time without any preparation. He was very sorry to hear about "the unfortunate incident" at her apartment. "I hope there was no serious damage, or anything of importance taken. It's always a shock when these things happen."

Regina tried to steady herself, not very successfully.

Without saying how he knew about the break-in, Brambilla went on as if he hadn't noticed any distress and, for that matter, had no doubt that the "incident" had something to do with "our shared interest."

"Our San Maurizio evidently likes to be a center of attention. Your researches, official investigations, art world ambitions in New York—they would like my picture to travel there by the way." He glanced toward its hiding place behind the wainscoting, then turned back to her. "More of Maurizio's adventures, we might say."

The light touch was not much of a distraction. She doubted it was meant to be. She could try to change the subject. Show annoyance at being used. Tell him what she had found out. She held back for what felt like ages.

"Yes, Maurizio's adventures. And Giotto's too." She could hardly leave it at that, then realized that she didn't want to. "But you wouldn't expect to find about either of them in Siena."

"Siena?" He sat up too quickly for his usual composure.

She took some reckless pleasure in saying more. "Drawings in Siena of a Maurizio figure. Together with a black man that looks like the one in the Arena Chapel. In Giotto's style."

Brambilla massaged his chin slowly. Poise finally restored, he rehearsed his own conclusions as if they were questions. "The style of Giotto, you say? Meaning not by Giotto himself? And the Padua figure and Maurizio on the same sheet—both black Moors?"

The Siena photos were in Regina's bag. After one last twinge of doubt, she brought them out and handed them to Brambilla together with a photo of the New York Maurizio that Phyllis Farber had released to the press.

"It depends on what to make of these. I saw them in a portfolio of an old time restorer in Siena. Duccio Chiarini. His daughter had seen my name in the papers. She wanted to show me that her father was a brilliant master of the old Tuscan styles. She wondered if these drawings might be studies for the New York picture that she had read about in the newspaper."

"I take it you must have agreed—that Chiarini was indeed *un gran maestro.*"

He sat back, extending the tips of his fingers towards her. "The New York people will have to say so too. To save face for being taken in." He paused with a confiding look. "When you tell them about Chiarini's splendid studies for their so-called Giotto."

He had hit exactly on what Regina had already decided she had to do. Taking her silence for agreement, he pressed further. "I believe you said that there are only drawings of a black Maurizio in the Chiarini album."

She was pretty sure he knew that she had not said that. And that she knew why it mattered to him.

His picture was under investigation; there were doubts about it. Without knowing quite how, or whether, to pose them, she had questions of her own about it. Having said enough, too much really, she gave him a disengaged "no others that I saw." That was true and there had already been too many revelations for the day.

Brambilla didn't pursue the point further, but she was left wondering whether San Maurizio might produce another miracle.

***

"*Parrocchia di San Maurizio,*" he repeated, shaking his head when Regina told him she was looking for parish records of the church of San Maurizio. The clerk in the archives of the Patriarchs of Venice was a youngish man who, as if stricken by an archivist's occupational disease, seemed to have aged prematurely. He looked startled to find her there. It felt like she was supposed to apologize for the intrusion until he handed her an application to consult the archive with a sigh of indifference.

The offbeat location and the quirky opening hours weren't encouraging. It figured that the high priests of Venice would house all but the most scandalous and incriminating records somewhere near San Marco. But Regina hadn't anticipated finding them across a little slip of a canal behind San Marco, in a rundown cloister with a random collection of religious paraphernalia, then after two sharp turns, up a nondescript modern stairwell to the third floor. The hours seemed—and probably were—designed to inhibit research.

"You won't find much of anything, but you can look in this," the clerk told her, pulling out one of a row of thick binders of inventories printed out on computer paper. She didn't expect to find anything; she had seen on line in her early searches that the only holdings for the parish were two baptismal registers dating from 1630 to 1760. In all the excitement of the last weeks she had forgotten about them, and it was only her last faint hope, or obsession, that brought her to the patriarchs' archives.

The only other researcher in the small reading room was an old man in a rumpled suit of no particular color who scowled at her and bore down on the scatter of papers on his table. One of the large dark paintings hanging on the walls represented, so far as Regina could tell, a throng of plague victims appealing for mercy. *Maybe I should try that,* she thought to herself as she filled out the paper request slips with a thirteen-digit call number from the inventory. The grizzled scholar ignored her conspicuously as he shuffled through his archival gleanings on old-fashioned note cards.

The large registers finally delivered by the impassive clerk—three instead of the two listed in the inventory—were composed of folio sheets bound in crumbling leather covers. Opening the first volume, Regina found a folded paper insert labeled "certain notices from the XIVth century." She did a double take until she saw that they were printed in the 18th century in the course of a sulfurous turf war between a rival parish's clergy and "the Most Reverend Priest of S. Maurizio." She was left, after all, with baptismal registers for 1630-1760, and not even the originals but 18th-century copies.

Leafing through the volumes, she recognized here and there some great Venetian family names, but page after page mostly recorded people known only by profession or place of residence. Countless infants were listed as baptized *in articulo mortis.* She had to steel herself from so much sorrow.

Giving up was one way of doing so, but before returning the registers to the clerk, she turned back to the introductory note she had skipped on opening the first volume. The author and compiler of the registers identified himself there in fluid cursive as Canciano Crovati, the incumbent parish priest of San Maurizio since 1750. He declared that he had assumed responsibility for listing the baptisms he had performed as well as those performed before his time. Some of his predecessors were "pious and worthy," but his Christian charity had limits. Other predecessors, he wrote, had left regrettably uneven and incomplete records. More lamentably still, nothing at all survived before 1630.

For in that horrendous year, registers, books, furnishings, everything had been destroyed by the fire that compounded the terrible miseries of the plague, and to which the priest Stefano Michieli also succumbed. May He Rest in Peace.

10

Scomparsa Clamorosa al Palazzo Bastagli: Il Capolavoro di Giotto. The glaring headlines broke the news that Giotto's San Maurizio had been reported missing, probably stolen, on the eve of being presented by Piergiorgio Brambilla to his grateful fellow citizens. The authorities were scrambling, promising an immediate investigation, "sparing no effort to recover the masterpiece and to see it returned to its rightful home." Phrases about "this extremely delicate and difficult mission" hedged likely failures.

Accusations of disgraceful official negligence, "as usual," were already flying. Insinuations bloomed into full-fledged conspiracy theories in letters to the editor: "Although he has pledged his cooperation, it is well known to many that Piergiorgio Brambilla's personal ambitions, in which the welfare of the city he has casually adopted is a minor consideration, always outweigh our collective needs."

Brambilla took the siege of rumors for what little it was worth. It would be obvious to everybody who cared that the Consorzio and its minions were trying to divert attention from their troubles with the law. The tactic was desperate and all too familiar.

They had it wrong, upside down. He did care about the city and didn't see his personal ambitions as a contradiction. Returning a Giotto San Maurizio to his church was a demonstration of patrician values, not at odds with civic commitments in the past or the present. It was old style Venetian, an offering and a promotion for a project that was his but also for the good of his parish and the city. Brambilla fancied the idea that Enrico Scrovegni would have approved.

This was why he had reported the picture missing and made sure it would stay put for as long as he chose. It had already served its purposes as a pledge of his good intentions; it would continue to do so in its absence without the danger of exposing the "difficult circumstances" of its acquisition.

Uncle Maurizio had spelled them out in the letter he left for his nephew with the painting in the Geneva vault.

> *My dear nephew, I was told that this hitherto unknown work attributed to Giotto came from a collection assembled and reserved for the highest German authorities. It was given to a friend by a high-ranking officer in the German Art Protection Commission that*

supposedly looked after our art treasures during the war. Toward the end of that horror, he resolved to safeguard artworks that might otherwise be stolen, damaged, destroyed. Or so he told my friend. A fine sentiment, no doubt, and useful for him too. He swore that he had waited until it was not suicidal, then refused orders to blow up the booty in his charge hidden away in mines, tunnels, cellars, and the like. Some German museum authorities cooperated; hoping not to be seen as Nazi collaborators, they calculated that the victorious allies would not dwell on the past of such estimable friends who, all along, had cared only for art. In turn, this officer took his own share for what he called his service to humanity and offered this picture to my friend, trusting in his discretion and his influential contacts to facilitate his escape until the true story could be told. Of course the truth could not be told. These were the "difficult circumstances" I once mentioned to you that induced my friend to ask me to keep the picture concealed. He died soon afterward. Now it is up to you to choose what its future shall be.

There was not much mystery about the "friend of a friend's" motives. When everything was coming apart in the last days of the war, he would have culled the picture from his cache of "saved" art to exchange for a favor, a bribe, or a passage to safety. Probably all of those things.

The picture had most likely come from Italy in the first place. German agents had combed, then ransacked the peninsula for art, the Jewish collections above all; the Fascists had little choice but to celebrate this as the latest barbarian tribute to Italian culture. The black girl's find in the archive suggested Scrovegni, Giotto's big patron in Padua, had left a San Maurizio painting to his parish in Venice. It all fitted well enough with a Giotto attribution.

Except for Chiarini. Brambilla had seen Regina Payne's photos of the drawings in the Siena portfolio; they looked like studies for the Maurizio painting, *maniera di Giotto*, in New York. Payne said she hadn't seen Chiarini studies of a white Maurizio.

He was sure that they must have existed. Under a magnifying glass he had detected tiny swastikas punched almost imperceptibly into the gold background of his picture. They were interspersed here and there with minute initials: DC, Chiarini's monogram. Regina Payne wouldn't have been looking for them before meeting Chiarini's daughter in Siena. The Germans either didn't see them, chose to ignore them, or, in their arrogance, took them as a prophesy of the Third Reich. But Brambilla understood now that Chiarini's exquisite contrivances exposed and mocked the lying blindness of the Nazis.

116

A stupendous achievement! Not one but two San Maurizios taken for Giottos. How unfortunate Chiarini's surpassing mastery could not be saluted here and now as it deserved to be. But that could change, and, with the benefit of time, *godendo il beneficio del tempo*, probably would change.

***

"About this picture business. I mean, give yourself some credit." Flavia was her assertive self. "Thanks to what you found out in Siena, Brambilla's picture wins out over the New York imposter. And now it's gone, probably already in some hideaway in Geneva or some oligarch's vault while cooling off. The joke's on Letizia Bassani's bosses; they'll fall over themselves trying to discredit Brambilla to having to help him find it."

They had agreed to meet at a distance from Campo San Maurizio after Flavia's yoga class. Flavia had objected at first. She brushed off the idea that they should look somewhere else for a studio. "You need to get back on track. Marcella's good and we're used to tuning out the babble. Anyway you're not going to worry in the lotus position."

That wasn't at all clear. The Campo had reverted in Regina's mind to its unredeemed state. Even Vivaldi sounded cheerless in non-stop muzak coming from the church; the reliefs on the misbegotten façade looked, as they had when she first saw it, like mannequins molded out of grimy wax. More painful to remember: the apartment with the green door where she had spent her last night with Giovanni.

It seemed ages ago. Seeing his name on a kiosk poster still triggered a shiver of regret. The most recent headline shouted out in boldface: *Giovanni Bonelli Leaving A. C. Milan??*

She had hoped that the attraction across their differences might somehow be bonding, but she knew all along that this was probably magical thinking. If it was a question of how and when a break would come, sooner would probably be better than later. She didn't want to believe that Giovanni was doing Brambilla's bidding to inform on her. Maybe he wasn't. But it would be pretending to suppose that his leaving A. C. Milan was some proof of that or that it had had anything to do with her.

Flavia surveyed the tables at the Café Foscarini. "I guess this place is far away enough away for you." It was surprisingly quiet and comfortable considering that it was just off the traffic coming to Dorsoduro across the Accademia bridge. "Anyway, poor Maurizio's Campo doesn't even rate a proper bar. And now it looks like his church isn't going to have his picture, either." Regina imagined all eyes turning toward her. Her conscience was roiling with the need to confess and be absolved.

She was being savaged for sabotaging Phyllis Farber's big San Maurizio stravaganza in New York. "Out of her depth, fatuous, no credibility

117

whatsoever." This was Farber's line: "The truth is that these Siena drawings are copies of our Giotto, not the other way around." Regina didn't stand much of a chance against a high-powered New York dealer's spin. And she couldn't be sure whose side Terterian was going to come out on.

Without her asking, Flavia picked a line of defense. "About that New York picture, the evidence is on your side from what you've told me. Your adviser's not going to cave to a dealer's pitch; he'll be discredited if you are. Giotto scholars will take sides, meaning that some will be on yours; arguing is what they do."

Regina did think that her hypothesis that a G.I. had smuggled the New York picture out of Italy as a souvenir war trophy would hold up. She might be able to confirm it with some further research.

As for Brambilla and his picture, its disappearance, oddly enough, was something of a godsend; it was not likely to turn up, not soon anyway. "Disappeared art" rarely did. Whoever took it wouldn't be foolish enough to market it but would keep it stowed away somewhere. That meant she could take her time deciding what to do.

She stopped. *But it doesn't matter much anymore. Everything in the church of San Maurizio burned up hundreds of years ago.*

***

Regina had decided to pay her respects to Giotto's Moor. It felt like the thing to do, a pilgrimage to the one-and-only that had inspired—if that was the right word—so much respect. She entered the Arena again through the side gate. It was still an inviting alternative to the obstacle course pretending to welcome visitors at the main entrance. She had not paid all that much attention before to the ruins, remnants, disappearances, restorations, recreations, and add-ons of different eras. The chapel, Giotto, then the Moor, were what mattered to her then.

It was different now. She couldn't separate the chapel from the layered histories of the Arena or Giotto's Flagellant from its afterlife. Least of all from her experience. Pilgrimages were about the trip as much as the arrival. Regina hadn't got what she wished for: an authentic black San Maurizio by Giotto and a brilliant dissertation for herself. But she hadn't ended up empty-handed in a fun house of fakes. She had been obliged to think through distinctions that seemed much too facile now.

Chiarini's note on his sketches about "inventing" a San Maurizio had gradually made sense to her. It didn't necessarily mean "making up" but something more like "finding" or "discovering." Regina knew that this was true of the saint in the first place. The relics, the sword, and the spear she had seen in Vienna were tied into imperial dreams—and nightmares—from Roman antiquity to Hitler; they were as real as the ambitions invested in them. For Chiarini to work like Giotto was an act of devotion more than a deception; his black Maurizio was just as black as the saint had been in the tradition that came down to Giotto and Scrovegni. Chiarini's white San Maurizio must have been a deliberate falsification, but it was the fake that exposed the truth of his white "Aryan" remake.

Regina was not altogether sure where this left her, but the open-endedness felt somehow like a liberation and a resolution. She liked to think that Scrovegni was something like that, free and resolute at the same time. Even in her first impressions he had never looked like a guilty penitent; he was a man who chose to contract with the Virgin and the saints, and with Giotto. The deal was not a payoff or a cover-up but a tradeoff, not a hypocritical variation on the Golden Rule.

Thinking about those first impressions now, Regina could see that they belonged to the early days of her coming to terms with art history and Italy too. She knew from the start that a black woman from Georgia who was serious about Renaissance art was not going to be an easy fit in America— and certainly not in Italy. Going native as some academic immigrants to Italy, even to Venice, vainly imagined they could do, was out of the question. But she could learn her way well enough to get around, even if her steps weren't quite right. And being an outlier afforded some protection. Regina didn't mind being enough of an innocent abroad to push back against Flavia, who always had to be right.

Even so, she had assimilated well enough to appreciate an Italian alternative to the default Italian position of disbelief. It wasn't resignation, though there were many Italian gestures for that, and it definitely wasn't innocence. It was something more like what Brambilla might have called in a knowing way "a certain justice." She remembered his Italian gesture that didn't signify "certainty" in the sense of judgments delivered once and for all.

She had come close to blurting out to Flavia what she had discovered about the fire. She stopped herself at the last minute; no good would come out of an ego rush or an absolution. There was no hurry after all. Let the truth come out when it would. Meanwhile, the investigations and plots against Brambilla would be diverted into a search for the "regrettable loss of a masterpiece" and time would reward him for "his magnanimous intentions toward his adopted city."

Justice could play out differently with Terterian. Regina had decided she had to tell him about the fire. That would make it easy for him to side with her about the New York San Maurizio. But there was more to it than that. Real scholars did not hide their research.

As it turned out, Terterian was grateful when she told him. "So, Regina, that takes care of the New York San Maurizio by Giotto aka Chiarini. And it gives me an easy way to get Phyllis Farber off my back. What a shame,

Phyllis,' I'll say, 'that Giotto's San Maurizio was burned up; a long time ago too. But we do have new masterpieces, by Duccio Chiarini. Chiarini's family will want yours back, but I'm sure you'll find a way to do the right thing.'"

"And the right thing for me?" Regina asked.

"Deciding for yourself. You could go back to the Bellini. But you've got another project now. 'New Masters for Old Pictures: Creative Anachronism in Renaissance Art.' You're already something of an expert and you'll have plenty of work to do in the best museums in Italy."

ACKNOWLEDGMENTS

This book, crossing boundaries between history, imagination, and shared experience, is not entirely a work of fiction and resemblances to actual events are not coincidental. The authors are grateful to friends in Venice who have welcomed them with a generosity that *foresti* can't take for granted and don't always deserve. Special thanks to Marina and Quico who have shared space, company, lore, and feasts at the Palazzo Barbaro. Frances Starn, Victoria Nelson, Lisa Kaborycha, Meryl Bailey, Katya Wesolowsi, and Jonathan Sheehan generously read drafts and are hereby absolved from any failure on our part to take full advantage of their thoughtful insights. We are grateful for TextFormations' highly skilled and tactful assistance with formatting and layout.